European Identity in Cinema

Edited by Wendy Everett

intellect™

intellect

EUROPEAN STUDIES SERIES

General Editor: *Keith Cameron*

Humour and History	Edited by Keith Cameron
The Nation: Myth or Reality?	Edited by Keith Cameron
Regionalism in Europe	Edited by Peter Wagstaff
Women in European Theatre	Edited by Elizabeth Woodrough
Children and Propaganda	Judith Proud
The New Russia	Edited by Michael Pursglove
English Language in Europe	Edited by Reinhard Hartmann
Food in European Literature	Edited by John Wilkins
Theatre and Europe 1957-1995	Christopher McCullough

First Published in 1996 by
Intellect Books
EFAE, Earl Richards Road North, Exeter EX2 6AS, UK

Series editor:	Keith Cameron
Production:	Rachel Carey
Copy editor:	Tess Moran

British Library Cataloguing in Publication Data Available

ISBN 1-871516-91-9

Printed and bound in Great Britain by Cromwell Press, Wiltshire

Contents

Preface: Filmic fingerprints   5

1. Introduction: European film and
    the quest for identity   7
    Wendy Everett

2. Framing the fingerprints:
    a brief survey of European film   13
    Wendy Everett

3. Louis Malle: a European outsider
    in the American mainstream   29
    Peter Hawkins

4. *Les Visiteurs*: a popular form of
    cinema for Europe?   35
    Anne Jackel

5. Wenders' *Paris, Texas* and the
    'European way of seeing'   45
    Stan Jones

6. Identity and the past in recent
    Russian cinema   53
    David Gillespie

7. The critique of reification:
    a subversive current within the
    cinema of contemporary Spain   61
    Dominic Keown

8. Current problems in the study of
    European cinema and the role of
    questions on cultural identity   75
    Ian Aitkin

9. **Film and Northern Ireland:**
    beyond 'the troubles'?   **83**
    Brian Neve

10. **Peripheral visions:**
    film-making in Scotland   **93**
    Duncan Petrie

11. **Timetravel and European film**   **103**
    Wendy Everett

Bibliography   **112**

Preface
Filmic Fingerprints
Wendy Everett

Fingerprints are tiny, unique traces of an individual identity; clues in which the most minute variations of a general pattern can make possible the identification, recognition, and reconstruction of that identity.

The essays in this book do not attempt to provide a history of European film, nor a detailed discussion of complex questions of national identity: such issues have adequately been dealt with elsewhere. Nor do they seek to provide an exhaustive account of European film production; instead, they offer a series of stills, or filmic fingerprints, of various aspects of European cinema, as part of an exploration of the complexities and diversities which lie at its heart. For it is clear that if we are to find a meaningful way of talking about European film, it will not be by imposing upon it a tight series of restrictive definitions. European cinema is not a monolith, but a series of expressions of different ways of questioning and portraying itself and the world. The differences must therefore be part of any analysis of its identity.

It is fashionable to decry Europe for its Eurocentrism; to attack its complacency (particularly in matters of culture), and to blame it for its traditional white, male, and middle class nature. Again, such is not the concern of this book. It leaves to others the task of saying what European film should be, and looks instead at what it is. However, this examination shows clearly that traditionally marginal voices are now at last being heard, and that films are vitally used as a means of exploring historical guilt and interrogating personal and national identities. Film is a fundamental part of the process of change that constitutes identity.

While this book does not investigate television production and the much heralded new information technologies, which, many estimate, may make film entirely obsolete within the near future, such issues do clearly impinge on any examination of cinema's present identity in so far as they add to the general pressures on directors and producers and contribute to cinema's current sense of unease. On the other hand, they may also enhance cinema's belief in its unique role in providing Europe with its own images and myths.

As film embarks uneasily upon its second century, Europe itself faces the doubts and uncertainties of the *fin de siécle*; this is a time of general reckoning and re-evaluation; it is a time of re-examining past histories in order to understand present problems, so as to be able to move forward in a positive way. Without this process of intense self-evaluation and transition, Europe would be doomed; a decaying post-colonial society, an irrelevance. Here we see curious echoes of the position of cinema itself; born more or less with this century, it has occupied a privileged position within modern European history; indeed, in many ways the two are inseparable. At the moment, the future of European film is uncertain, and this is revealed by its own search for identity in films which are increasingly self-conscious and self-reflexive. Faced with the massive domination of Hollywood at both production and distribution levels, as well as the coming technological revolution, threatened by financial problems whose very solutions increase its vulnerability, even if European film does exist, how much longer will this be true? And does it matter?

Contributors to this work provide a varied range of approaches and responses to such questions, yet all share a basic conviction that European cinema does matter to Europe, and what emerges in these essays is a clear indication of the fascination and complexity of the subject.

I should like to thank my family for their support; Keith Cameron (General Editor of the Intellect European Studies series) for his patience; Peter Wagstaff for his help and advice; and, of course, all the contributors for their ideas and enthusiasm.

Introduction
European film and the quest for identity
Wendy Everett

Understanding and defining what European means involves an obsessive wrestling with contradictions, suspicions, and uncertainties. In 1991, Pierre Sorlin prefaced his book, *European Cinemas/European Societies*, with the affirmation that even if, 'culturally, [Europe] is a patchwork, a juxtaposition of various conceptions and practices of entertainment, a collection of individual ways of singing, dancing, telling stories, practising sport and having some rest', that is to say, a heterogenous and fragmentary collection of distinct individual identities, at least 'economically and even politically Europe is already a reality'.[1] A mere three years later, such certainty had vanished, so that in his study of European regionalism, Peter Wagstaff could cite the vulnerable status of economic and monetary union, and the increasing controversy surrounding several of its essential features, such as a single currency, to support the view that 'The goal of political union remains no more than a hazy outline in the distance, fast disappearing over the horizon'.[2] The events of 1995 have so far done nothing to contradict this view.

Indeed, it seems increasingly clear that the suspicion and prejudice that have for so long divided our small nations cannot easily be forgotten, resurfacing repeatedly in political wranglings, and reflected in headlines of various national newspapers. Even the optimism that followed the fall of the Berlin wall and the end of the cold war has been impossible to sustain in the face of unspeakable horrors of territorial conflict and ethnic cleansing. Instead of growing closer, European nations seem to be drifting further apart, in the current of political fascism and xenophobia; while the creation of a popular mythology of Europe as monster preying upon national sovereignty and identity has further served to highlight difference.

In other words, now as always, Europe is a fragile construct, 'an archipelago of diversities',[3] an uncomfortable juxtapositioning of irregular shapes, whose outlines do not match, and are themselves, in any case, always in the process of becoming something else.

On the one hand, whilst we can identify numerous political, historical, and cultural elements which unite European nations, shared references which suggest some possible understanding of what it means to be European, on the other, we are perpetually reminded of the crucial differences which divide us. Faced with underlying diversity and heterogeneity, we are perhaps justified in wondering whether any definition of Europe other than the strictly geographical is possible, and even that of course has become particularly problematic in the unstable aftermath of the disintegration of the Soviet bloc, and given the profound structural changes which characterise postmodern geographies in general.[4]

Given the constant need to re-evaluate and reassess past and present which is one of the consequences of such processes of change, it is not surprising that questions of identity, whether personal, national, or indeed European, should have assumed a particular importance in recent years.

1. Sorlin, P. (1991), *European Cinemas, European Societies, 1939-1990*, London: Routledge, p.3.
2. Wagstaff, P. (ed.)(1994), *Regionalism in Europe*, Oxford, Intellect, p.1
3. Compagnon, A. (1992), 'Mapping the European Mind', in Petrie, D. (1992), *Screening Europe*, London: BFI, p.108.
4. Morley, D. and Robins, K., 1981, p.21-25

The fundamental issue of whether, in cultural terms, Europe has any meaning or identity other than diversity and difference, provides a context for this book's examination of the role and status of cinema in Europe; each of the essays which follow focuses upon ways in which films are used to interrogate, to express, or possibly even to construct, identity.

Whilst talking about European film must, of course, immediately raise all the above problems of divergence and conflict, it is clear that film itself occupies a significant, even privileged, position in contemporary European culture. Born more or less with the century which now draws to its close, the cinema has always seemed uniquely able to express its concerns. Filmic images have mirrored the major events which have marked the twentieth century; have investigated its harshest realities; and have increasingly shaped the way in which we Europeans see ourselves. In other words, the twentieth-century history of Europe and that of its films are inextricably linked, and as Europe now stands poised on the brink of an uncertain future, so too does cinema.

If, as we have already seen, it is impossible to reach a definition of European in political, economic, or even geographical terms, and if the cultures of Europe can be recognised primarily by their differences, then it is not surprising that a search for the identity of European film should present us with a daunting range of problems. Not least because film itself is structured by contradictions (mimetic and fantastic; realist and escapist; challenging and entertaining; artistic endeavour and/or industrial product), but also because of the basic complexities involved in creating and recognising cultural identity.[5]

This book raises a number of important issues. First, can we reach any understanding or definition of the nature of European cinema, and if so, how is it possible, and what might such an understanding involve? Second, in what ways might our understanding of the identity of European film make possible a deeper understanding of the basic questions of European identity?

Not surprisingly, given the complexity of the whole issue of identity, contributors to this volume reveal a range of different approaches. However, central to all the essays is the belief that there should be no attempt to present identity as monolithic or unproblematical, since 'the search for a stable and coherent identity can be successful only at the expense of repressing internal differences, tensions, and contradictions'.[6]

One approach, adopted by Ian Aitkin in his study of European cinema and cultural identity (chapter 7), is to use the theory of globalisation as a framework in which differences can be categorised and examined. He thus avoids prescription or limitation, instead listing the themes and issues which predominate, and showing how these reflect cultural and political change, and how they relate to national issues of identity.

Another approach to questions of identity is the recognition of the role of the foreign in defining the national: 'that a cinema or broadcasting network or a discourse of advertising is British because it is not French or German or North American'.[7] This is the stance adopted by Morley and Robins in their analysis of the nature of cultural identity: 'cultural identity must be defined in relation to differentiation from other cultural identities'.[8]

The possibility of defining oneself as other emerges clearly in our

5. Anderson, B. (1983), *Imagined Communities*, London: Verso/Hay, D. (1968), *Europe, The Emergence of an Idea*, Edinburgh: Edinburgh University Press/Higson, A. (1989), 'The Concept of National Cinema', in *Screen*, vol. 30, no. 4, Autumn 1989, pp. 36–46.

6. Ibid., Higson, A., 1989, pp. 36–46

7. Cubitt, S. (1989), 'Over the Borderlines', in *Screen*, vol. 30, no. 4, Autumn 1989, pp. 2–8.

8. Morley, D. & Robins, K., 'Spaces of Identity: Communications Technologies and the Reconfiguration of Europe', in *Screen*, vol. 30, no. 4, Autumn 1989, p. 10

General Survey (chapter 2): national myths and constructs, not to mention the fraught questions of language difference, enable us easily to characterise one or other of the national cinemas we study. However, this book traces a more complex identity, that of European film, itself composed — as we have seen — of contrast and differences. Can clues to this identity also be found by concentrating upon what sets it apart from other world cinemas?

Such an approach enables one to group individual national differences on one side of an equation in which the opposing term is non-European film. In this instance difference itself is used to provide a framework in which to explore the concept of European film. European film is not American film; to put it another way, the European notion of film, its status, and its function, is essentially different from that of the United States. An attempt to understand identity through differentiation, underlies both Peter Hawkins's study of Louis Malle, a director who, unusually, seems to have succeeded in straddling the American and European systems without compromising his French, or European identity, and Stan Jones's analysis of Wim Wenders' film *Paris, Texas.*. It was through directing this film and its immediate predecessors, in America, in English, that Wenders finally confronted the differences that enabled him to define himself once and for all as a European director, and indeed to return to Europe to work.

Where might we begin to pinpoint such differences? Three major elements made Wenders aware of his otherness, and caused him to acknowledge that he could never become an American director: the first was linguistic, by not using his language, he was losing his identity; the second was method, his way of filming (his need for overall control in a small team of technicians with whom he specifically and repeatedly chose to work provoked perpetual discord in the States, where it was not the norm); and finally both the content and the style of his films was fundamentally different from American films.

Such concerns, in fact, are generally presented as basic to any analysis of the problematic nature of identity,[9] both in theoretical discussions, and pragmatically.[10] For instance, the importance of making films in a nation's own language emerges in almost all the essays in this volume; it is seen as a prerequisite to any representation of national identity, and as the key issue for traditionally marginalised nations.

Language difference is, at the same time, one of Europe's greatest obstacles to creating a profitable American-style film industry, and it is presented in this light by Anne Jackel, as one possible reason why *Les Visiteurs* was, despite its director's attempt to produce a film with international appeal, generally unsuccessful outside France (chapter 4). Equally, language difference is a fundamental consideration in the whole question of co-productions, which might otherwise suggest a useful way forward for European directors; this issue is also examined in the General Survey, and in Duncan Petrie's analysis of Scottish films (chapter 10).

Methods of filming at once lead us to the often emotive question of *auteur* cinema, and its traditional relationship with notions of film as art. It may well be unfashionable to talk in terms of the *auteur*, yet it is clear that virtually all the directors discussed in these essays would see themselves in this way. (Moreover, as Peter Hawkins points out, we are currently

9. Schlesinger, P. (1987), 'On National Identity: Some Conceptions and some Misconceptions Criticised', in *Social Sciences Information*, vol. 26, no. 2, p.234.

10. This might be compared with, for instance, Compagnon's list of distinguishing features: common reference points (historical and geographical); shared concepts; common aesthetic values (see Compagnon, 'Mapping the European Mind', in Petrie, D. (1992), *Screening Europe*, pp. 106–113).

witnessing a move in the States to an *auteur* approach, in the work of directors such as Spielberg and Tarantino.) It is equally true to claim that it would be impossible to confuse even a few seconds of, for example, Wenders and Tarkovskii, or Buñuel and Almodóvar. Whatever the financial and other pressures, such directors make films which are entirely personal, in an entirely individual way. And this simply does not tie in with a large studio system or with attempts to produce big budget, commercially successful films. This debate is, as we shall see, central to European film-making today.

Finally, and closely related to the method of filming, is the question of style and content. The majority of European films are not afraid to be provocative and challenging, and to require a creative response from their spectators; there is a strong tradition of independent, personal filmmaking in Europe that supports this view, and the vast majority of European directors see their films in these terms, and are generally resistant to the demands of mainstream Hollywood.

Thus, it is clear that recognition of difference can provide a framework within which positive indications as to what European film is can be established. In other words, we can see that beyond the differences and contrasts, there might well be shared aims and concerns that constitute European film.

Let us return for an instant to Malle who, although successfully working in English and in French, in Europe and the States, still sees the nature and role of his films to be quite fundamentally different from that of mainstream Hollywood. As Peter Hawkins shows, Malle's films are concerned with marginality and difference, and are posited upon the value of the individual. Malle, like his protagonists, refuses to conform to the dictates of his class and society, but seeks instead to challenge and disturb. His films are subversive, not particularly in their style and technique (although they are more innovative than is generally recognised), but in their subject matter and its treatment. For Peter Hawkins, Malle is a European director precisely because he positions himself as an outsider, and thus is able to challenge the viewer's perceptions of society.

To what extent is this implicit definition of European film valid? Widely, if we consider the essays in this book. European films remain healthily sceptical of society and government. Their ironic gaze seeks to provoke, challenge and to disturb. This is clearly illustrated in Dominic Keown's analysis of three major Spanish directors: Buñuel, Berlanga, and Almodóvar, all of whom, he suggests, believe their role to be that of Spain's conscience, as they attack, with ironic and often savage humour, the utilitarian and monetary value placed upon the individual by a capitalist society. These directors want to open the spectators' eyes to their condition; to provoke a critical awareness; their films are essentially subversive.

The notion of film opening the spectators' eyes is of central importance, and the critical gaze of European film is as likely to be directed inwards, upon subjective landscapes, as outwards, upon society. In the current uncertainties which shape Europe, filmic discourse frequently interrogates the nature of reality, identity, and — in particular — memory. In his study of contemporary Russian films (chapter 6), David Gillespie notes how, since the 1960s, directors have increasingly turned to the past, in search of understanding, and in order to reflect upon the events and people that have shaped the present. Such films repeatedly pose, whether explicitly or implicitly, the same questions: How did all this happen? Who is to blame? Where do we go from here? It is essential to recognise that the nature of film is a fundamental constituent in this process of interrogation; an inextricable part of the ongoing, open-ended process of reassessment and change: a feature which is widely recognised by directors right across Europe. This aspect is the key to Wendy Everett's essay on time travel; film is the ideal time machine, the very nature of its language enabling it to recreate processes of memory, and thus to become part of the subjective, ironic, continuous interrogation of personal and indeed European identities.

Film therefore both reflects and creates identities; both reveals and composes the myths and images which shape European vision and European identity. Within the self-conscious autobiographical explorations of memory which Wendy Everett notes, this duality is reflected by ways in which film itself provides both the object and the means of the quest for identity. Perhaps this is what explains, in part at least, the particular significance which newly formed, or especially vulnerable societies accord to film. In our General Survey, this point emerges repeatedly, linking countries as divergent as Iceland and Wales; film images, like the language in which the films are made, are essential to the expression of national identity. In David Gillespie's analysis of identity and the past in Russian film, we see how Russia, now groping towards an uncertain identity, turns to culture and the cultural consciousness (of which film is an essential part) in its search. In his essay on film making in Scotland, Duncan Petrie discusses the importance for Scotland of having an indigenous film industry, after years of seeing itself only through other nations' eyes. His wide-ranging survey of recent film-production in Scotland ('the cultural and economic peripheral centre of what is a marginalised entity') provides a useful indication of the enthusiasm and dynamism which characterise attitudes to film in places which have been traditionally marginalised and silenced.

Brian Neve, in his study of the complex nature of representation in the cinema of Northern Ireland, particularly addresses the issues of marginalisation, within the specific social and political problems of that country. He questions the ability of its films to challenge the stereotypical images which are a legacy of its marginal status and of its traditional representation by, in particular, the British media. His study emphasises the importance of film in raising and questioning fundamental issues of identity, a point which further reinforces the idea that European films actively seek to affect issues of identity by analysing, challenging, and criticising dominant ideologies and beliefs.

This brings us back to the complicated issues of national identity and nationalism. If film is seen by struggling, new, or marginalised societies as essential to the creation of a national voice, might this suggest a breaking away from the European ideals of closer union and understanding? The picture of fragmentation which results is one which Aitkin fits into his globalisation framework, claiming that the rapidly accelerating transnational environment causes individual societies to feel increasingly vulnerable, and to choose fragmentation and isolation. However, it is also clear, and in

European terms, hearteningly so, that such countries while breaking away from those which have traditionally dominated them, actually turn towards Europe whose diverse and multifaceted nature offers less of a threat to their own identity. 'Scotland's relationship with Europe, both past and present, allows space for the articulation of identity which is necessarily hybrid, diverse, and outward-looking', writes Duncan Petrie.

Are European films, concerned with such complex issues, therefore doomed to remain on the fringes, in the art house cinemas so widely criticised by those who seek a more profitable film industry? There are certainly considerable pressures to change the situation, and these are examined in the survey, and in Anne Jackel's analysis of *Les Visiteurs*, in which she comments that 'for many cinema goers, the terms European and popular have become incompatible'. Such concerns are, of course, endemic in the 'film as art or entertainment' debate which, sadly, continues to dominate critical thought. It is important that this debate should not be allowed to falsify the situation by suggesting that popular and serious film are somehow incompatible. If the making of films is as central to European identity as these essays suggest, then surely they will exhibit the same diversity and variety that characterises all cultural forms. As such, Anne Jackel's belief that comedy, for example, tends to be ignored by European critics, at least, unless it is American comedy, is worrying. But, of course, humour, and ironic comment, are to be found in almost all European films, no matter how serious; indeed one of Baudrillard's defining differences between America and Europe is that in America, 'the irony of community is missing'.[11] Interestingly, John Caughie too posits irony as a characteristic (perhaps the only common characteristic) of European cinema.[12]

What all this suggests is, perhaps, that there is a marked vitality and sense of purpose in European film, despite the many problems which beset it, and that the various fingerprints it leaves on the pages of this book provide both ample proof of its existence, and fascinating indications of its identity; multifarious, complex, and elusive as it may be. For if film is to provide the means of exploring and representing the cultural heterogeneity of Europe, and the complex processes of change which this involves, then there is no point in seeking a single and limiting definition. 'America has no identity problem' writes Baudrillard;[13] Europe does, and its films explore the endless complexities of that problem, whilst becoming part of the identity which it seeks.

11. Baudrillard, J. (1988), *America*, London: Verso, p.85

12. Caughie, J. (1992), 'Becoming European: Art Cinema, Irony and Identity', in Petrie, D. (1992), *Screening Europe*, London: BFI, p.36

13. op.cit., Baudrillard, J. 1988, p.76

Framing the fingerprints: a brief survey of European film

Wendy Everett

In the hundred years since its invention, cinema has played a central role in European life, offering, in turn, escape and entertainment, intellectual and artistic challenge and vitally, a means of questioning and expressing identity and individuality, and of creating national myths. Film has provided solace in times of hardship, has served as political tool and as subversive weapon, has been exploited as propaganda and gagged by the censor. Film reached its apogee in many European countries in the grim aftermath of the Second World War, when audience numbers soared and cinemas provided an important community focus and social function, whilst the films so fervently viewed offered audiences a shared set of images of the world. Since then, the importance of cinema has declined and its prospects are regarded as bleak although, ironically, the need for film as exploration of historical difference and expression of national identity has, in many ways, never seemed more important.

The picture is a mixed one: while the number of cinemas in Europe has declined steadily since the 1950s, along with the percentage of the population regularly going to see films, there are indications that this trend may now be changing. Moreover, increasing sales and rentals of videos confirm that films themselves are still perceived as important, even if the social connotations of watching them are different. What is certain is that, like fast food chains, American films now massively dominate the European market. If we consider, for example, the main box office successes of 1993-94, the extent of this domination becomes clear.

Jurassic Park tops the list, for instance, in Austria, Belgium, Britain, Denmark, Finland, Germany, Greece, Hungary, Iceland, Ireland, Italy, Luxembourg, The Netherlands, Norway, Poland, Slovakia, and Spain; that is to say, in all but three of the European countries for which these statistics were available. Incidentally, in the three 'exceptions' it still came second, after *Aladdin* in France and Sweden, and after *Sister Act* in Switzerland. Even if we expand the list to include the ten most popular films, the situation scarcely alters; in very few European countries do domestic, or other European, films fall within this category.[1]

The reasons for this situation are complex. The professionalism of American movies is, of course, important, as is the fact that they are generally made according to a successful commercial formula. They aim to attract a mass audience by providing dramatic narrative, pace, and escapism, and they represent a fashionable modern viewpoint to the younger generation. However, the conclusion that their overwhelming success is merely a reflection of consumer choice is somewhat simplistic.

European film-makers today face two major problems: the first is funding, the second, closely related, is distribution. Distribution networks are controlled by an ever decreasing number of companies, most of which are American owned and therefore promote American films. Indeed,

1. Statistical information for this chapter has been gained from a wide range of national publications provided by various national film institutes and academies, and from various guides to contemporary film, the most useful of which are indicated below.

Europe constitutes a highly desirable market for film, America's second most profitable industry.

Inadequate publicity and distribution systems for domestic films means that they are unlikely to reach the attention of the general public. This means that potential audiences are thus restricted, and chances of financial success are slim, irrespective of the quality of the film. With little prospect of large scale profits, directors find it impossible to obtain adequate financial backing. European films are almost inevitably small budget productions, a fact which undoubtedly damages their image amongst home audiences, for whom media concern with the enormous budget of popular American films may imply that cost and quality are inseparable.

The consequences are clear: as Europeans have less access to the films which purport to represent them, and are instead nourished with somewhat bland mainstream Hollywood, they feel increasingly alienated from the slower more reflective language of European cinema.[2] Clearly, this matters to directors who are under pressure to produce more commercial, less 'European' types of film, if they wish to survive; for European audiences the consequences are a matter of continued debate. However, if film does offer a means of questioning notions of identity, involving self-awareness and development, and if it is true that they are our chief access to reality, given that 'our relationship with events and people is mediated by images; some we produce for ourselves but most are assigned to us by the society we live in and are therefore common to virtually all members of the group', then globalisation and the loss of specifically European images will indeed have serious consequence.[3]

The context of the increasing dominance of American films thus provides the first of the elements which all European countries share. Its impact is revealed initially in European film's attempts to define itself by what it is not. In other words by its difference from classical Hollywood film: strong and unambiguous narrative, fast rhythm and action, star system and sophisticated special effects. Thus, European directors often consider their distance from these concerns in identifying their own specificities such as irony and self-consciousness, playfulness, slow, reflective camera work, challenging editing, open-endedness and refusal to offer solutions to the issues they explore.

The second consequence of the American monopoly is the increasing pressures on European directors to compete with Hollywood on its terms; to modify their work, so as to achieve larger profits, and to attract, in particular, the expanding young audience sector, that is to say, to deny their European voice.[4]

The various responses to such pressures are central to the future of European film. Should directors agree to emulate Hollywood, by reducing the number of films being made in favour of a few large budget productions, and by making films which closely mirror their American counterparts? Certain countries in general, and certain directors in particular, are moving in this direction, although, as yet, without necessarily increasing either their audiences or their profits. Indeed, the idea that merely imitating Hollywood will provide a universal solution to European problems is somewhat simplistic, not least because of the cultural and linguistic

2. As Luc Mollet points out, America tends to export its rubbish to Europe, not its more challenging films. Mollet, G. (1995), 'La toupie, Vigo et le coupe-ongles', in *Cahiers du Cinéma*, no 491, May 1995, pp.44-45.

3. Sorlin, P. (1991), *European Cinemas, European Societies, 1939-1990*, London: Routledge.

4. Thomas, N. (ed.) (1994), *Film and Television Handbook 1995*, London: BFI.

differences which, as we have seen, characterise Europe's widely divergent markets.

Alternatively, should directors and producers ignore such pressures, and instead insist that what Europe is good at is producing complex, challenging films which, by definition, will never attract a mass audience, but which are nevertheless of vital importance in allowing a nation to examine and voice its own identity?[5] It is clear that this response has serious financial implications: its tacit acceptance of the notion of film as art necessitates some form of subsidy, a solution which not all European governments are willing or able to provide. On the other hand, it has been widely argued that in fact, small budget films do not need to make vast profits to be deemed successful, so that perhaps what needs to be changed are the criteria for evaluating success rather than the films themselves.

A further increase in the number of co-productions, specifically European co-productions, is often posited as a compromise solution, or a way forward. It is true that many smaller countries are finding this development helpful, since costs are shared, and it becomes possible to make more films. However, it must also be acknowledged that co-productions have not so far proved a guaranteed recipe for success; indeed, the inevitable watering down of differences, and resulting blandness of these films, suggests to many that they are the worst of all possible solutions, 'compromised vehicles'.[6] Problems generally crystallize around language. Despite the fact that smaller countries see the use of their own language as essential to their representation, co-productions are frequently made in English so as to appeal to a wider audience.[7]

Clearly, such concerns are basic to any discussion of the identity of European cinema, and the various responses they elicit will provide important pointers within the debate. It is perhaps comforting that merely by suggesting that European film should change, its critics are acknowledging that it does indeed possess an identity. Moreover, despite these problems, exciting and challenging films are still being produced throughout Europe. Many smaller countries are in the process of creating their own film industry and this proves that European voices are still believed to be worth fighting for.

> For film both reflects and refracts; it both mirrors and interprets the society which we inhabit, and our responses to it.

Vigdís Finnbogadóttir argues the case for Iceland to develop an autonomous film industry.[8] Widespread belief in the importance of national voices and European images, indicates the special status of film in Europe, and it is with this in mind that we shall begin our wider survey.

Clearly, in a short chapter such as this, only a limited amount of information can be provided. For the purpose of coherence, representative countries will be examined within three categories, although here, as in Europe itself, divisions must be recognised as artificial and problematic. The main countries in the first group (Britain, France, Germany, Italy, Spain) have long-established domestic film industries and despite certain differences of attitude, reveal much common ground. It is important to compare their reactions to current problems, and to identify the focus of

5. See for example Hodgson, P. (1995), 'Pleurnicherie pour le cinéma français', in *Cahiers du Cinéma*, no. 489, March 1995.

6. Horton, A. and Brashinsky, M. (1992), *The Zero Hour: Glasnost and Soviet Cinema in Transition*, Princeton: Princeton University Press.

7. Almodóvar, P. (1992), 'A Propos du cinéma espagnol', in *Cahiers du Cinéma*, no. hors-série, 1992, p.30.

8. Finnbogadóttir, V. (1993), 'A Challenge to Achievement', in *Icelandic Films 1993*, Reykjavik, The Icelandic Film Fund.

current filmic debate and any recent changes in modes of film production which may indicate important new trends.

Each of these nations has, as we have said, individual film traditions dating back at least to the early years of this century, as well as a history of shared points of reference and influence. In this, Spain can be seen as something of an exception, since its protracted isolation under Franco protected it from many of the common European experiences:

> For decades the Iberian peninsula lived in isolation, ignoring the transformations and crises the other countries went through [9]

However, since the 1970s, film in Spain has experienced a dramatic transition,[10] which has given birth to a new generation of film-makers, aware both of their filmic heritage and of their affinity with the rest of Europe, and whose work is characterised by what Victor Erice described as a new 'spirit of discovery'.

Of course, freedom of expression is always fragile. If Franco stifled the voicing of national (and regional) concerns in Spain, giving the State unlimited powers of censorship for nearly forty years,[11] so too did Hitler, and then the Allies in Germany, Mussolini and the Fascists in Italy, and the Vichy government in Occupied France. The cinema is particularly vulnerable to censorship, and this emerges most clearly in times of war or when democracy is under threat; there is a certain irony in noting that at present Britain has the strictest regulations in Europe. The predominant relaxing of censorship is most dramatically illustrated by the new freedom of directors in the former Soviet bloc, and by the 1994 decision of the Netherlands to abolish censorship entirely. However, media pressure in Britain has led to tough new government restrictions limiting the general release not only of feature films, but also of video.

Moreover, as we have seen, domestic films and national voices are also threatened by American hegemony in all of these countries. The dangers are perhaps most clearly seen in Britain which is, in any case, possibly the least European of all European countries, given that its population as a whole considers its allegiance (filmic or other) to be with America rather than Europe. Many of the problems of the British film industry result from the so-called special relationship which Britain and the United States have shared, and from their common language.[12] The results are clear: a distribution network massively dominated by standard American fare, reflected by the fact that nineteen of its top twenty box office successes for 1993 were American (Kenneth Branagh's *Much Ado About Nothing* being the exception); while outstanding films such as Ken Loach's *Raining Stones*, a film which does express British concerns, might well have attracted reasonable audiences in Britain had it received the publicity and distribution automatically accorded to American films.

But in fact, Britain is not alone in this matter, Germany also has a long history of American dominance. Thomas Elsaesser traces this back as far as the end of the First World War, but American interests gained absolute power in Germany after the collapse of the Nazi regime, when economic objectives were used to complement political goals.[13] By the early 1950s, German cinemas were saturated with American films, and a German national cinema seemed impossible; and it is easy to find historical reasons

9. Sorlin, P. (1991), *European Cinemas, European Societies, 1939-1990*, London: Routledge, p.21.

10. Hopewell, J. (1986), *Out of the Past: Spanish Cinema after Franco*, London: BFI.

11. Molina-Foix, V. (1977), *New Cinema in Spain*, London: BFI, p.4.

12. Roddick, N. (1985), 'If the United States spoke Spanish, we would still have a Film industry', in Anty, M. and Roddick, N. *British Cinema Now*, London: BFI.

13. Elsaesser, T. (1984), 'Putting on a Show: The European Art Movie', in *Sight and Sound*, April 1994, pp.22-27.

for that situation. The fact that Germany is once again dominated by American films is more worrying however, and the situation seems to be deteriorating. Writing in 1989, Elsaesser could point out that, despite the problems facing German film production, the number of domestic entries at the Berlin festival was increasing.[14] However, in 1994, there were only three: Reinhard Munster's *Back to Square One*, Michael Gwisdek's *Farewell to Angels*, and Lienhard Wawrzyn's *The Blue One*, none of which won any prizes. Moreover, no German films were even entered at Cannes. In 1989, Germany was producing 80-100 films a year, but by 1993-4, the total had fallen to 67, of which 17 were international co-productions. Indeed, in 1994, only one 'German' film *The House of the Spirits*, made it into the top ten box office successes (in eighth position). Since this film was a German/Danish/Portuguese co-production, directed by Bille August, and made in English with an international cast, it can hardly claim to represent German identity. The situation in Italy is similar: film output is falling, so that the 50 or so feature films made in 1993-4 represent a 20% decrease from the previous year and, apart from Bertolucci's *Little Buddha* (a co-production filmed in England, and scripted in English), no Italian films featured in Italy's top ten in 1993 or 1994. The situation in Spain is no better, indeed having joined the European Community in 1988, Spain has particular financial problems as it struggles with competition from both America and Europe, and film production is falling steadily. One of Europe's most popular and successful directors, Almodóvar, has managed to avoid pressures on his films by setting up his own private company. He believes Spanish film is currently the most vulnerable in Europe.[15]

While France confronts the same basic problems, it still manages to produce more than 150 films each year, a third of which may be first or second features, as well as being involved in some 70 co-productions, and giving financial support to Eastern European directors. Indeed, France's film industry is probably still the most dynamic in Europe, in terms of both quantity and quality.[16] How is it possible to account for this different response to the same problems and pressures that face Britain, Germany, Italy, and Spain?

The most obvious reason is funding. It is almost a cliché these days to talk about the crisis in British film, since its entire history has been marked by chronic underfunding:

> Anyone with even the remotest interest in the British film industry will know that it is in an almost permanent state of financial crisis.[17]

On the other hand, the GATT triumph enabled the French to retain their *Fonds de soutien*, a system whereby subsidies are granted to French film-makers through a tax levied on all cinema tickets sold; and further funding is provided by television channels. However, it would be naive to account for the different responses merely in these terms. Germany too has a system of subsidies (state and federal), based on a tax on cinema admissions yet, as we have seen, film production there is far from healthy. While subsidies are not therefore the whole answer, they are nevertheless important, and both Spain and Italy are in the process of developing new systems, primarily to encourage young directors. However, whatever the system chosen, the finance available is always likely to be inadequate.

14. Elsaesser, T. (1989), *New German Cinema: A History*, London: BFI, p.309.

15. op.cit., Almodóvar, P. (1992), p.29.

16. Ciment, M. (1995), 'France', in *Variety International Film Guide*, London: Hamlyn.

17. Petrie, D. (ed.) (1992), *New Questions of British Cinema*, London: BFI.

In fact, the issue of funding reflects a more fundamental consideration, namely the status which a nation accords to its films. By 1916, Canudo's definition of cinema as 'the seventh art' had been widely accepted in France, and despite fluctuating fortunes, this basic appreciation of film still holds there, accounting, in part at least, for its relatively secure status. When, for example, French (and European) directors fought to be excluded from the GATT agreement on the grounds that film is a cultural product rather than an industrial one, they received almost unanimous support from across the French political spectrum. This is a situation which would be unthinkable in Britain, where film has traditionally been regarded as an inferior form of theatre, as entertainment for the masses, excluded from the grants accorded to the other arts. 'The granting of social respectability was unnaturally delayed for the cinema in Britain', comments Perry in his history of British film.[18] Indeed, the conflict between film as art or industry still prevails in Britain, which retains its suspicion of the 'artiness' of European film, and where audiences tend to be particularly polarised in their choice of viewing, a situation which David Puttnam sees as inevitably detrimental to the industry as a whole:

> British cinema has for decades been driven by an endless and largely sterile debate revolving around the thesis of art versus commerce.[19]

Whilst it is likely that Puttnam himself has frequently contributed to this debate, being more than a little critical of film which makes a 'personal (frequently obscure) statement',[20] it is true that this basic uncertainty as to the status of film renders it particularly vulnerable, as is shown by its current problems in Britain, and indeed, in Germany.

One of the consequences of film's vulnerability is that directors are pressurised to make Hollywood-style movies, and are therefore discouraged from making low-budget, experimental films. While French directors are better able to withstand such pressures, if they choose, nevertheless many directors do attempt to make films with a mass appeal. *Les Visiteurs* may in many respects be seen as one such attempt which did succeed in France, as will be shown in Chapter Four. However, if European films desire American-scale profits, they must attract Europe-wide audiences and, as we have seen, this is difficult. The general 'failure' of *Les Visiteurs* outside France, provides useful material in the ongoing debate about the nature and future of European film, since it raises linguistic issues (to dub or to subtitle), as well as cultural characteristics such as humour, highlighting the individual specificities of European nations, rather than their unity.

Problems may be further compounded by the increasing fragmentation of national film industries. The development of national cinemas by, for example, Wales and Scotland, make any discussion of 'British' film increasingly problematic. Similarly, references to 'Spanish' film appear to exclude the significant output of Galicia, the Basque country, Valencia, the Canaries and, above all, Catalonia. As later chapters will reveal, this subdividing of national identities is a widespread feature of contemporary Europe. What is, perhaps, of particular significance is that, as such 'minority' voices strive to be heard, they turn away from the dominant national culture, and towards Europe, for support, so that paradoxically, this apparent fragmentation may well constitute a strengthening of the notion of

18. Perry, G. (1974, p.9)
19. Puttnam, D. (1974), 'Foreword', in Perry, G. (1974), *The Great British Picture Show*, Toronto, Little Brown and Company, p.6.
20. Ibid.

European film. Certainly, it reinforces the conviction that European films matter, and let us consider why, by looking at their major concerns.

Whilst it is possible to identify a preoccupation with history and identity as central to the development of European film, it is clear that the second half of this century has seen a shift towards an increasingly subjective representation of history.[21] Even here, nevertheless, important differences mark the films of individual nations. In Britain, the most commercially successful films are currently period pieces and literary adaptations. Whilst it is tempting to fit these into the general European concern with history, memory, and identity, they can more correctly be seen as an attempt to escape from present problems to a safer, grander past. Comforting, nostalgic, and visually pleasing, they are marketed as part of Britain's cultural heritage, a sort of filmic tourist industry which Thomas Elsaesser sees as a form of cinematic prostitution.[22] However, 'heritage films' such as *Much Ado about Nothing* (Kenneth Branagh, 1993); *Howards End* (James Ivory, 1991); *Peter's Friends* (Kenneth Branagh, 1992); *The Remains of the Day* (James Ivory, 1993) and *The Crying Game* (Neil Jordan, 1992), have found a firm niche in the market, and are often quoted as examples of successful 'crossover' films, in that they can make the important transition from minority to mainstream audiences.

German films also look backwards in time, but with little risk of nostalgia or complacency. As Sorlin points out, Germany appears to be the only European nation not yearning for the first half of the century.[23] Whilst this is a generalisation, it is true that the guilt and pain of Germany's memories of the Third Reich meant that it was later than most other countries in openly exploring memory and history in its films. It was not until the late 1970s and 1980s that German directors really confronted the past, in films such as *Hitler ein Film aus Deutschland* (*Hitler, A Film From Germany*, Hans Jürgen Syberberg, 1977), and *Die Ehe der Maria Braun* (*The Marriage of Maria Braun*, Fassbinder, 1978). Until then, for the most part, German film had favoured the security of literary adaptation, remake, and pastiche, and these genres remain popular. Now, however, the problem of history is central. What happened to, and in the name of, the Germans between 1933 and 1945, and how it affected and continues to affect Germany and the rest of Europe, is still so incomprehensible that it is at the core of any attempt to define German identity. Sorlin suggests that Germany could approach its history only gradually and partially, citing, as an example, the fragmented structure of *Hitler*; one could also view Kluge's *Die Patriotin* (*The Patriot*, 1979) in these terms.[24]

If this relatively distant event has received a disproportionate amount of attention, it is because the Second World War and its aftermath still constitute a central point of reference in European film, as indeed in Europe. Whether war emerges in exploration of national or personal guilt, as in Bertolucci's *Il Conformista* (*The Conformist*, 1971) or Louis Malle's *Au revoir les enfants* (1987), or in nostalgic childhood memories, as in Boorman's *Hope and Glory* (1987), its scars are still raw, and it is clear that establishing closer European ties depends in part on the ability to reassess former divisions and concepts. It is therefore interesting that Susan Haywood identifies a lack of history in recent French films; tracing a development from history as 'dissimulation' (1960s), to 'revelation' (1970s), and

21. See Chapter 11
22. Elsaesser, T. (1994), p.26
23. op.cit., Sorlin, P. (1991), p.183)
24. See Chapter 11

'diasporisation' (1980s).[25] However neat the formulation, which she bases on an image of contemporary France as 'ideologically asleep' and on the assumption that historical films are avoided because expensive and unlikely to become blockbusters, it ignores the notion of history as progress and as point of view that Sorlin recognises. Yet the more intimate and subjective form of historical film, most clearly illustrated by filmic autobiography, is a significant European development. France is no exception, with its tradition of personal film, dating back at least as far as Astruc and the New Wave movement. One exciting initiative which recognises the important relationship between personal memories and history was recently set up by *Arte* (the cultural television channel), which commissioned nine different directors each to make a film based on her/his adolescence. The series includes André Téchiné's *Les roseaux sauvages* (*Wild Reeds*, set in the early 1960s, at the time of the Algerian war); Olivier Asseyas's *L'eau froide* (*Cold Water*, dealing with teenage rebellion in the early 1970s); Patricia Mazuy's *Travolta et moi* (set in the mid-1970s), and Chantal Akerman's fascinating *Portrait d'une jeune fille de la fin des années 60, á Bruxelles* (*Portrait of a girl in the late 60s, in Brussels*). The intimate visions of history these films offer, and their notion of memory as a process which actively influences present and future, support Hopewell's recognition of the importance of cinema in recalling and reassessing the past. Films such as *The Long Day Closes* (Terence Davies, England); *My Ain Folk*, (Bill Douglas, Scotland) and *Caro Diario* (*Dear Diary*, Nanni Moretti, Italy), reaffirm the European tradition of film as personal statement, and illustrate convincingly the importance of small budget, independent films which have the freedom to explore such issues.

Another of the shared features of European film is a concern with present day social issues and marginalised voices. In Italy, for example, many current films deal with social questions ranging from the continuing Mafia threat (Guiseppe Ferrara's *Giovanni Falcone*), to regional problems of poverty and unemployment (Gabriele Salvatores's *Sud* (*South*).

Recent reactions to the extreme right wing Italian government include the formation of a number of politically subversive film groups. One such, led by Nanni Moretti, produced for instance a short film called *L'Unico Paesi al Mondo* (*The only Country in the World*), as an attack on Berlusconi's power; while films by Silvio Soldini and Maurizio Zaccaro deal critically with issues of racism and immigration. These themes also predominate in Germany (where social problems caused by unification are still acute), in works by directors such as Gunther Wallraff, and in Britain, in films by Stephen Frears or Ken Loach.

European films thus freely explore uncomfortable ·social and moral issues and are not afraid to criticise official attitudes. However, it was suggested earlier that one of the defining characteristics of European films is innovation and experiment; a refusal to conform to the prescribed rules of classical Hollywood, with regard to form as much as to content. If European film is to retain its vital role, it must therefore continue to experiment and develop. Given current pressures to conform to popular mainstream Hollywood, is there any evidence that innovation and experiment still survive in European films?

There is, of course, a preponderance of safe genres: historical romances,

25. Haywood, S. (1993), *French National Cinema*, London and New York: Routledge, p.285

unadventurous comedies, action movies and, in particular, literary adaptations; films with a strong narrative, likely to appeal to a reasonably wide range of spectators and, in the case of the last category, films whose cultural respectability seems assured. So far, however, Europe has retained the personal, small budget film, which is free to subvert filmic conventions, and to risk shocking the spectators. Indeed, a healthy industry is one in which a wide variety of types of film can flourish. It is clear that in countries with long traditions of filmmaking, established voices will tend to dominate; however, this need not necessarily imply a lack of innovation. In France, even established figures such as Godard, Malle, Rivette, Chabrol and Resnais, continue to surprise. An obvious example of this being Resnais's *Smoking/No Smoking*, an adaptation of Alan Ayckbourn's *Intimate Exchanges*, in which Resnais, with typical cinematic playfulness, forces the spectators to make choices and to accept creative responsibility for the film. Jean-Luc Godard continues to challenge perceived filmic parameters in films such as *Hélas pour moi*, while his latest release, *JLG/JLG*, makes a further contribution to the autobiographical genre we have already noted; this is particularly interesting, given Godard's previous reluctance to discuss his childhood.

In Germany, on the other hand, with the exception of a few young directors, amongst whom are Pepe Danquart and Katja von Garnier, there is little recent evidence of innovation. Even Wenders's recent *In weiter Ferne, so nah* (*Faraway So Close*, 1993), a sequel to *Der Himmel über Berlin* (*Wings of Desire*, 1987), failed to arouse public enthusiasm, and the domestic film industry is clearly in crisis.

In Italy, established directors, such as Ermanno Olmi, Alberto Sordi, Franco Zeffirelli, Liliana Cavani, and Guiseppe Tornatore, continue to dominate the screens, often making it difficult for younger directors to have their work shown. But these younger directors are widely successful in European film festivals, and Italy appears to retain its belief in the importance of its films.

British directors wishing to make challenging or unusual films, face endless financial struggles, and the knowledge that their films will remain on the art cinema circuit, out of sight of most people. *Ladybird, Ladybird* (1994) illustrates this. It is the first of Ken Loach's films to be given a wide release in Britain since *Kes* (1969), but despite its enthusiastic European reception (including the International Critics Award at the 1994 Berlin Film Festival), British audiences were small. However, such films support the argument that European directors should not attempt to compete with Hollywood, because their talents and interests are better expressed in more intimate and small scale productions. Other British directors whose work falls into this category include Terence Davies, Peter Greenaway, John Boorman, Derek Jarman, and Bill Douglas. Although their films do not make vast profits, they do challenge perceived filmic language, and offer an honest exploration of the nature of British, or indeed European, identity; they thus constitute an essential reference point in the European debate.

Many of the above comments also apply to Greece, where the production of domestic films is decreasing under financial constraints. Currently, about ten films are made each year, and despite measures to increase the funding available to Greek directors, it seems unlikely that this number will increase much.[26] However, whilst American films, dominate the screens here, as elsewhere, Greece's pro-Europeanism is reflected by widespread interest in films from other European countries. Therefore, alongside the ubiquitous *Jurassic Park*, films by Kiéslowski and Almodóvar, for example, featured in the main box office successes of 1993–94. As in Spain, there are signs of a new spirit in the cinema, and here too, its role in reassessing and coming to terms with Greece's troubled past is central. The Greek Film Centre's new production programme, New Perspectives, created to facilitate the making of low budget features, has played an important part in encouraging young directors such as Pericles Hoursoglou and Sotiris Goritsas (joint winners at the National Thessaloniki Film Festival in 1994), and Antonis Kokkinos.

Greek films reveal familiar concerns: marginal voices are represented in, for example, *From the Snow* by Sotiris Goritsas, an exploration of the Balkan tragedy from the point of view of two members of Albania's Greek minority; while memory and history are dominant themes, revealed in such films as *Lefteris* (Pericles Hoursoglou), *I Dream of my Friends* (Nikos Panayotopoulos), and *A Starry Dome* whose director, Costas Aristopoulos, uses the Oedipus myth as a framework for an individual journey through collective artistic memory. The films of Theo Angelopoulos too, for example, *O Melissokomos* (*The Beekeeper*, 1986), can be seen as critical journeys into the past, as recurrent explorations of memory and identity.

Austria, Belgium, Luxembourg, Portugal, and Switzerland, are smaller nations whose film output has tended to be overshadowed by their larger and more powerful neighbours. They are countries for whom internal linguistic differences frequently add to the problems of commercial distribution that are a common feature in Europe. As a result, they have remained somewhat isolated; many directors have made their films elsewhere (Godard, Varda), and those who remained, with a few exceptions (Delvaux and Straub in Belgium, Gorretta in Switzerland) are not widely known outside their native countries, so that the threat of Hollywood domination is increased.

On the other hand, Portuguese film, starting from a similar base, is experiencing something of a rebirth, largely thanks to the new Portuguese Institute of Cinematographic and Audiovisual Art (IPACA), which is strenuously promoting Portuguese film at home and abroad. Lisbon was named the Cultural Capital of Europe in 1994, and one of the results was an increase in the film budget. The IPACA financed four of Portugal's six feature films that year; three of these were selected for Cannes and, tellingly, the April 1995 edition of *Cahiers du Cinéma* devotes an entire section to Portuguese film.

The next group of countries to be considered comprises the Scandinavian countries: Denmark, Finland, Iceland, Norway, and Sweden. Again the group may seem strange, in that it links Iceland, one of the youngest of the European film industries, with Sweden, which has for a long time been one of its most important. However, it is clear from all their official documentation and publicity material that Scandinavian film industries have chosen to co-operate closely. A significant aspect of this group is its attempt to define a group identity within the wider European

26. Bouquet, S. (1995), 'Les hérauts du cinéma grec', in *Cahiers du Cinéma*, no. 490, April 1995, pp. 14–15

context, without sacrificing the national linguistic and cultural differences. Between them, these five countries produced 56 feature films in 1993, and contributed to a further 18 offshore co-productions. Whilst American films predominate here as elsewhere, domestic films remain popular, accounting annually for between 28% and 15% of the films viewed, while films from the rest of the group, and from other European countries, also figure widely.

Clearly, this situation is relatively encouraging, and it is important to identify what sets Scandinavian film apart. Significantly, Sweden, with its long film history, suffers most from the problems noted earlier: its distribution circuits are dominated by American movies, and there is limited enthusiasm for its domestic films. Sweden's solution is to increase to over 50% the number of Nordic co-productions being made there, with support from the Nordic Film and Television Fund.

For a long time, the Swedish film industry was seen as synonymous with the work of Bergman. His films are of course seminal to any understanding of European film, not least in helping to establish the tradition of using film to explore personal memory, for instance in his semi-autobiographical *Fanny och Alexander* (*Fanny and Alexander*, 1983), but the work of other directors is becoming increasingly familiar outside Sweden. One example is Lasse Hallström, whose semi-autobiographical *Mit Liv Som Hund* (*My Life as a Dog*, 1987) was popular throughout Europe; his latest film, *Kadisbellan* (*The Sling Shot* 1994), also autobiographical, promises to do the same. Bergman's influence continues in *Söndagsbarn* (*Sunday's Children*, 1993), in which Daniel Bergman explores his father's memories of Dalarna in the summer of 1926, and in Bille August's film of Bergman's account of his parents' courtship and early marriage, *Den goda viljan* (*The Best Intentions*, 1992). Swedish directors such as Suzanne Osten consider social issues such as racism, immigration, and inequality, illustrating again film's important critical function. Therefore, while sharing the problems and preoccupations of other well-established film industries, Sweden continues to make interesting films, but increasingly in partnership with other Scandinavian countries.

The basic problems of American hegemony and lack of finance are compounded in Finland, Norway, Denmark, and Iceland by the minority status of their national languages. Given that language is a key to individual identity, the obvious solution to financial problems, an increased participation in co-productions, is complicated by the fact that international support inevitably requires films to be made in English. As Marianne Möller points out, writing about Finnish film:

> This is problematic because one of the aims of domestic film support expressly is the promotion of Finnish language productions.[27]

The hope of avoiding an English language takeover is fundamental to the development of Nordic co-productions.

The success of Scandinavian films is revealed by their increasing appearance at European film festivals, and the work of many directors is now widely recognised. The Finnish brothers Aki and Mika Kaurismäki, for instance, have made more than twenty features in the last fifteen years. Their quirky low budget films brim with nihilistic humour and the width

27. Möller, M. (1993), *Suomen Elokuvasäätiö Vuosikertomus, 1993*, Helsinki: Suomen elokuvasäätiö.

and diversity of their filmic references, ranging from Godard to Finnish and Hungarian traditions, certainly contribute to their widespread popularity. One of their best known films is *Leningrad Cowboys go America* (1989), which follows an inept sixties-style Finnish pop group on a disastrous tour of America.

However, it is Iceland, one of the newest of all European film industries,[28] that presents the most positive profile, for although few films are made each year (scarcely surprising given the size of the population), these are exciting and are received enthusiastically by home audiences. Indeed, Iceland's belief in the importance of film is expressed by its President, Vigdis Finnbogadóttir:

> ...in a world where film has become a truly international language, no society can consider itself properly articulate until it can express itself through this most contemporary of media.[29]

Land and Sons examines the collapse of traditional social and cultural values and the transition from rural to urban economy, during the Second World War. It was made with financial backing from the newly created Icelandic Film Fund. While the money was minimal, it was enough to get the industry started and such factors must be considered relevant to the European subsidy debate. Television too has helped to encourage new talent, by offering experience to aspiring directors.

Iceland in fact has the keenest cinema goers in Scandinavia,[30] and their enthusiastic response to seeing their own films in their own language initially brought great financial success. Now that the novelty has faded, audience numbers are falling, and the industry faces severe debt; in 1993-94 only two new feature films were made: *Hin helgu vé* (*The Sacred Mound*, 1994) directed by Hrafn Gunnlaugusson, and *Bíódagar* (*Movie Days*, 1994), directed by Fridrik Thór Fridriksson. It is interesting that both films are semi-autobiographical, and that both have proved as popular elsewhere as they have in Iceland. Indeed *Movie Days*, Fridrik Thór Fridriksson's third feature film, is Iceland's most successful film export ever. It is composed of the director's fragmented memories of childhood, and of Reykjavik in 1964, slowly coming to terms with the changes that followed its occupation by British and American forces.

In conclusion to this section, we can note that Scandinavian films all have access to some form of state subsidy and that, even when inadequate, this has enabled the industry to survive. Moreover, the decision to co-operate has enabled Scandinavian countries to form some defence against American dominance, particularly against the English language. Success is greatest where film offers a new means of expressing national identity, but there is enthusiasm and a sense of purpose everywhere.

Our somewhat disparate final section includes small countries or regions which have traditionally been denied a voice in film, and countries whose new independence results from the disintegration of the former Soviet bloc. The key feature which links them is a passionate belief in the importance of film as expression of national identity and difference; linguistic and cultural specificities thus preponderate. This concentration on difference may appear ironic in the context of European integration and solidarity; however, it is important to recognise that for the Welsh, the

28. Iceland's first film, *Land og synir*, (Land and Sons), dates from 1979.
29. Kristinsson, A., Pálsson, S., and Pálsson, S.S., (eds.)(1993), *Icelandic Films 1993*, Reykjavik, The Icelandic Film Fund, p.4.
30. Ibid.

Scots or the Basques, for instance, the threat to identity has come from the larger states to which they have belonged. Europe, whose essence is diversity, appears to offer co-operation without the threat of domination, and they therefore tend to look towards Europe more positively than the longer established film industries do.

In such countries, film is important because it expresses national identity; accordingly, there is considerable enthusiasm for domestic films, particularly if they are made in the native language or dialect. Duncan Petrie's chapter provides a detailed picture of recent film production in Scotland, and notes the positive reaction of the Scottish public. Although fewer films have appeared in Wales, the response has been terrific, above all when they are made in Welsh. *Hedd Wyn* (Paul Turner, 1992) provided a turning point, being the first Welsh language film to be awarded an Oscar. Moreover, the story of the poet Ellis Evans, killed in the trenches in 1917, and posthumously awarded the bardic chair at the National Eisteddfod, is part of Welsh mythology, and expresses many of the beliefs fundamental to Welsh identity. The industry continues to flourish, largely thanks to the creation of the television channel Sianel Pedwar Cymru (S4C) in 1982, which provided a lifeline for young Welsh directors.

Independent production is now healthy, with centres in Bangor and Caernarvon in the north, and Cardiff in the south. In 1993 the Welsh Film Council was set up, with promise of more adequate levels of funding, whilst the recently created Screen Wales provides support for marketing and distribution. New developments include the creation of a national film archive, and a film school, and there are a number of film festivals across the country. It is interesting that Wales, like Iceland, is a country with a strong literary tradition, where film has only recently begun to play a cultural role.[31]

Europe does, after all, accord a special importance to images of itself in its films; it sees the cinema as the most direct and powerful source of such images. One of the traditional problems of countries such as Scotland and Wales, is that the images of them that have traditionally dominated have been those created by outsiders.

> It was sobering to reflect that almost all the popular films of the thirties and forties which conditioned the way people outside Wales saw the nation, were made by outsiders.[32]

Similarly, writing about Ireland, John Hill comments that whilst there has never been any shortage of representations of Ireland and the Irish on the cinema screen:

> The source of these images, however, has rarely been Ireland itself. In the absence of any sustained output from an indigenous Irish film industry, it has been the cinemas of Britain and the United States of America which have been responsible for the vast majority of films to have dealt with Ireland and the Irish.[33]

It is seen as essential to create your own images of the world and of yourself, in your own language. Perhaps the strongest indication of the centrality of this image-making process emerges when we look at the various countries in Eastern Europe, many of which, both socially and

31. Berry, D. (1994), *Wales and Cinema: The First Hundred Years*, Cardiff: University of Wales Press, p.9.
32. Ibid.
33. Hill, J. (1988), 'Images of Violence' in Rockett, K. and Hill, J., *Cinema and Ireland*, London: Routledge, p.147.

economically, are still in crisis and struggling to survive in the wake of the collapse of communism. The dilemma facing film makers here results from the fact that they have been forced to confront both the unprecedented freedom of expression which followed the dismantling of state control, and the harsh commercial realities of funding and distribution. Writing about problems facing older Hungarian directors in the 1990s, Tibor Hirsch comments:

> Those who mistook the former artificial political and economic shelter for the natural film business environment, now feel trapped and severely disappointed,

and clearly this remark applies to all the former communist countries.[34]

Some countries have coped successfully with this process of transition: Poland, for example, with its long tradition of high quality films, already had a reasonably successful structure of film units, which it transformed into independent film studios. Moreover, it established a number of different sources of funding, both state and private. Polish television also encourages young directors, co-producing or commissioning 30-40 feature films a year, many of which obtain a cinema screening. The Film Art Foundation runs a nationwide network of art cinemas, as well as organising film festivals and events. However, this apparently positive picture must be placed in the context of widespread poverty, falling audiences, and an influx of American films which are very popular with Polish viewers.

Hungary too has a long and rich cinema history, but unlike Poland, it lacked both the money and the infrastructure to deal with recent events, and the present situation is bleak and confused, as audiences turn to American films, and directors find that private sponsors are endangering their new independence. State television is in crisis, and attempts to set up funding for young directors are slow to advance.[35]

The situation in Russia is equally confused. Many cinemas have been closed, and American films increasingly dominate the distribution circuits, now accounting for over half the ticket sales. It appears that only 14% of Russians currently view Russian films, which can be made only with foreign financial support. Russian cinema needs to understand and express difference and plurality and this involves redefining its priorities and its subjects.[36] In other words, after years of control, it must take on the difficult task of establishing an independent identity. However, the central importance of cinema within the wider changes the state is undergoing, is widely recognised, as the fact that some 70 films are made each year demonstrates. Indeed, there is talk of a second wave of directors, including Valery Todorovsky, Sergei Debizhev, Dmitry Meskhieu, and Sergei Livnev, all of whom made second features in 1994.

On the other hand, countries such as Bulgaria struggle with outmoded legislation, and severe poverty and inflation, making it astonishing that any films appear at all. Not surprisingly, recent films, such as Peter Popzlatev's *Neshto vav Vuzdouha* (*Something In The Air*, 1993) and Mihailov's *Sezonut na Kanarchetata* (*Canary Season*, 1993) show Bulgaria re-evaluating its recent history, in its search for its contemporary identity.

The expression of individual identity through a national cinema is also of vital importance to the tiny Baltic republics of Estonia, Lithuania and

34. Hirsch, T. (1994), in Bakonyi, V. (ed.) (1994), *Hungarian Film Guide, 1994*, Budapest: Tamás Varga, pp.4-16.

35. Ibid.

36. op.cit., Horton, A. and Brashinsky, M., 1992, p.5.

Latvia. Their enthusiasm is revealed by the recent proliferation of independent film studios (more than thirty in Latvia, for example), but unfortunately no infrastructure exists to support funding and distribution. Moreover, lacking formal protection, the domestic market has been swamped by American films and videos. Systems of control and licensing are gradually being created and, interestingly, these are based upon the Scandinavian model. Yet again, many of the films being made deal with time and memory, and explore the moral and spiritual values central to notions of identity.

Elsewhere, problems are even greater. The fact that Serbia and Slovakia, for instance, are still making films is a measure of the importance they accord to this activity. Even Slovenia, which has existed as an independent state only since 1991, makes two or three films a year, despite the lack of structures or funding, and the fighting which continues to tear it apart. Main categories of film in all these countries include literary adaptations, and representations of contemporary history. For example *Migrations*, made for television and cinema by the Serbian director Igor Luther, and described as a kind of Serbian *War and Peace*; and *Halgato* by the Slovinian director, Andrej Mlakov. This film is set amongst the gypsies on the Pannonian Plains near the Hungarian border, and explores questions of cultural tradition, identity, and marginalisation.

It is not surprising that Croatia's film industry has all but disappeared. Serbian agression has resulted in devastating damage and extreme poverty. But Croatia's belief in the importance of national language and culture as a means of ensuring its survival has never been stronger, and there is widespread conviction that film is central to expressing and preserving national identity, perhaps more important now than ever. Two films were made 1993, an achievement whose enormity is underlined by an article entitled 'In Front of the Cracked Mirror' written in 1994 by the young Croatian director Zrinko Ogresta, in which he wonders whether he will ever again be able to make a film, given the horrors he has witnessed: the destruction of his country, the death of his friends and colleagues. Drawing an analogy between his position and that of Croatian directors in the years following the Second World War, he wonders whether time will heal his wounds too. Ending with a quotation from Schiller, 'To forgive is to rediscover something of oneself which has been stolen', the article clearly shows a conviction that film, through its ability to express pain, can begin the processes of understanding, healing, and forgiveness without which there can be no future. This belief is shared by all European countries, and perhaps accounts for the very special position which, despite all the problems, film holds in the European conscience. Zrinko Ogresta's article also puts many common European problems into perspective, at least for John Boorman:

> When Zrinco Ogresta's piece landed on my desk, it threw all our problems with the movie industry into sharp relief.[37]

37. Boorman, J. and Donohue, W., (eds.) (1994), *Projections 3: Film-Makers on Film-Making*, London: Faber and Faber

This survey can only conclude that European film is curiously tenacious; against all the odds, there is a fundamental belief in its importance as part of Europe's search for its own identity, even if this cannot be equated with financial success, or even mass audience appeal. Indeed, this apparent dichotomy will be found at the heart of many of the essays which follow, in their explorations of the nature of European film. It is certainly true of the first of these, where Peter Hawkins deals directly with issues of funding and popularity, as they affect Louis Malle, and where he introduces another of the salient features of European film: its compulsion to question the society from which it stems, to disturb the viewer, and to provoke a critical and creative response.

Louis Malle: a European outsider in the American mainstream

Peter Hawkins

The notion of a European cultural identity is an elusive one — Europe seems still to be a *Europe des patries* in cultural terms, despite the development of Europe-wide policies in the audio-visual media. The recent conflict of interest between the United States and the European Union on the question of film and television products, and their place in the GATT negotiations, has nonetheless focused interest on the issue of the differences between the predominantly commercial American products and the distinctive cultural identity of the European ones. The French Government, of course, took the lead in defending the right to '*l'exception culturelle*' in this domain, and media products were in the end excluded from the agreement. This was greeted with sighs of relief in many quarters, and not just in France.

A point that emerges from this crisis and its resolution is that it is probably easier to formulate what a European cultural identity in cinema might mean by contradistinction with the cinema of the United States, rather than on its own terms and in isolation. To illustrate this proposition, the example of Louis Malle should provide a helpful case history. Malle offers us the example of an eminent film director who has made successful films on both sides of the Atlantic; whose films have focused on very American subjects, as well as very French ones; who has one foot in the 'art-house' market but has also enjoyed several big budget commercial successes and who has regularly used the facilities of European co-production, starting long before they were institutionalised, as long ago indeed as *Vie privée* (*A Very Private Affair*, 1961), and as recently as *Damage* (1992). It will be necessary to range widely over his filmic output in order to draw together the threads of the argument; an approach which, clearly, precludes detailed concentration on any single illustration. I shall nonetheless limit my references to his best-known films, and shall situate the points I am making in relation to particular films, by providing brief introductory descriptions of them. Although such an approach has the disadvantage of excluding Malle's extensive, but less familiar, output of documentaries, ultimately it is his most successful feature films which will provide the most telling examples.

In looking at the films of Louis Malle from the point of view of a hypothetical notion of 'Europeanness', two main areas of interest suggest themselves. The first concerns the choice of subject-matter of the films, their thematic content and, more importantly, the angle from which they are treated. The second area would seem to be his working methods as a director, extensively debated in the numerous interviews he has given, particularly the one published recently in book form by Philip French.[1]

It is a critical commonplace to comment on the heterogeneity of Louis

1. French, P. (ed.)(1993), *Malle on Malle*, London: Faber and Faber. See also various filmed and televised interviews, such as 'My Dinner with Louis' (with Wallace Shawn), BBC *Arena* , BBC, BBC production,1985, and 'Talking to Louis Malle' (with Philip French), Channel 4, Wall to Wall production, 1992.

Malle's films.[2] He does not seem to have any single identifiable style, and appears chameleon-like in his ability to absorb himself into a foreign environment, as his American films such as *Pretty Baby* (1978) or *Atlantic City* (1980) reveal. Looking at the body of his feature films, it seems to me that there is nonetheless a theme which runs through all of them, and that is marginality. It is shown through the status of an outsider figure or figures, and their relation to the norms of the society around them, which are often represented as corrupt or hypocritical. This marginality is even, to some extent, reflected in Malle's own status as an outsider within the French cinema — a precursor of the New Wave; often pigeonholed within that movement, but never actually having been a member of the *Cahiers du Cinéma* group alongside Godard, Truffaut, and company.[3] The son of a well-to-do French bourgeois family, he is nevertheless in constant revolt against its conservative values.[4] He is an anti-establishment film-maker, who has frequently been accused of reactionary tendencies, particularly with regard to his sympathetic presentation of a wartime collaborator in *Lacombe Lucien*.[5] Virtually all his feature films reproduce a similar dialectic of marginal figure at odds with a corrupt society, from the nihilistic, suicidal, right-wing and opportunist heroes played by Maurice Ronet in his early films, *Ascenseur pour l'Échafaud* (*Lift to the Scaffold*, 1957) and *Le Feu follet* (*A Time to Live and a Time to Die*, 1963), through to the rural Peter Pan figure played by Michel Piccoli in *Milou en mai* (*Milou in May*, 1989). Another example is from the bored and dissatisfied upper-class wife who runs away with a 2CV-driving archaeology student in *Les Amants* (*The Lovers*, 1958), to the emotionally damaged Anna Barton who wreaks havoc in the private life of a successful MP in *Damage*. This dialectic is directly relevant to our discussion, in that Malle himself appears to exemplify, both in his own career and in the subject-matter of his films, the importance of marginality, the value of the individualistic ferment in relation to a social norm which is always flawed in its conformity. Malle, like his heroes, appears to consider himself a marginal, anti-establishment figure, whose role is the constant disruption of the complacent bourgeois consensus.[6]

Could the same be said of European cinema in relation to its big brother across the Atlantic? Few European films manage to escape the ghetto of the art cinema circuit in North America, if only because they are either dubbed or sub-titled, a format apparently unacceptable to American audiences. Even on their home territory, European films now have only a minority share of the market in virtually all European countries. The big box-office battalions are always, it seems, the latest American super-productions, whether *Jurassic Park* or *Aladdin*, and most European films seem unable — or unwilling — to compete in the same league. The budgets accorded to European films are almost always modest in comparison, and their aims more individualistic and personal.

Should this be a cause for despair and defeatism? Not necessarily, I would like to argue. The number of European films which have been the subject of Hollywood re-makes in recent times, from *Breathless* (1983) to *Three Men and a Baby* (1987), suggests that European cinema performs an essential, inspirational, role for the North American mainstream. European film-making seems to provide a necessary yeast for the dough-production of Hollywood. Nor is it simply a question of scenarios and re-makes: the

2 Ibid., p.xiii.
3 Ibid., pp.30-31.
4 Ibid., pp.2-4.
5 Ibid., p.100
6 Mallecot, J. (ed.)(1977), *Malle par Malle*, Paris, Editions de l'Athanor.

status of the individualistic *auteur*, as exemplified by a figure such as Louis Malle, appears an exalted artistic role model to which the ambitious Hollywood director now aspires. Even a 'golden boy' such as Steven Spielberg, has a craving for the status of *auteur*, as he admitted to Jeremy Isaacs in a BBC Late Show interview in January 1994. His most personal film to date is the Oscar winning *Schindler's List* (1993), a black and white treatment of a subject not very far-removed from those of Louis Malle: the sympathetic portrayal of a Nazi war profiteer who redeems himself by saving Jewish holocaust victims.

By performing this role of free-wheeling outsider, Louis Malle is in a position to question the prevailing moral or social consensus, in much the same way as the independent investigative journalist or television reporter. In this respect, Malle's feature films are not far removed from his documentaries. Indeed, whether by upsetting the received view of the innocent resistance sympathies of *la France profonde* (deepest France) during the Occupation, or by questioning the simplistic anti-clerical assumptions of the complicity of the Catholic Church in the persecution of Jews during the same period in *Au revoir les enfants* (1987), Louis Malle's independent approach to film-making has proved its value, and has illustrated in an exemplary fashion just how effective European cinema can be as a disturber of comfortable consensus.

It is important to consider some of the ways in which Malle has achieved this subversive and disturbing quality in his films. What is immediately striking, is that his effectiveness in this respect is not limited to his own home territory. He can prick the conscience not only of bourgeois France, but also, quite remarkably, he is able to perform the same role in cultures quite different from his own. In the glossy historical costume drama, *Pretty Baby*, for instance, his amoral and sympathetic presentation of a brothel in the red light district of New Orleans in the 1900s shocked puritanical middle America. Their outrage was certainly compounded by his casting of glamorous Brooke Shields, as a fourteen-year-old child prostitute who eventually becomes the wife of a naïve and voyeuristic photographer (a role which, in fact, launched her subsequent career). Ironically, this subversive production was entirely financed by the Hollywood studio, Paramount. In a similar vein, Malle was able to play successfully with the images of a quintessentially American location in *Atlantic City*, a typically amoral account of two no-hopers getting rich on the proceeds of drugs stolen from the Mafia. The effects of Malle's disturbing critical eye are not, however, restricted to France or the United States, his adopted home from the mid-Seventies to the mid-Eighties. His documentary, *Phantom India*, provoked an outraged response from the Indian government in 1968, which subsequently forced the BBC to abandon its showing on television. His recent film, *Damage*, despite some narrative inconsistencies, and an ultimately unconvincing portrayal of destructive passion, nevertheless managed to present a persuasive and prophetic image of the weaknesses of the smug British political establishment, and also to do well at the box office, not merely in art-house cinemas.

It is interesting to observe how many of Malle's touchstone outsider figures are children on the verge of adolescence. At that age they seem to have sufficient worldly wisdom to see through the hypocrisies of their milieu, and yet to have preserved enough innocence and vulnerability to capture the audience's sympathy, and to carry them along in a process of discovery and demystification.[7] I have already mentioned Violet, played by Brooke Shields in *Pretty Baby*, and the lengthy list includes the irrepressible Zazie in *Zazie dans le Métro* (*Zazie*, 1960), and Laurent in *Le Souffle au coeur* (*Dearest Love*, 1971), whose sexual initiation culminates in a spontaneous and innocent act of incest, as well, of course, as the protagonists of *Lacombe Lucien* and *Au revoir les enfants*. All these characters view the conventional world of the adults around them from a privileged critical standpoint, and are not yet caught up in the the compromises their elders have accepted. They are thus the ideal vehicle for Malle's unsettling vision, above all since they are able to sustain the spectators' sympathy.

It seems to me that independent non-conformism is a function which the most memorable European cinema has always performed to a very high degree of sophistication, and that the films of Louis Malle provide a convincing demonstration of this. However, it is perhaps not enough merely to identify the moral or aesthetic role of European cinema, vital though this is. Given the current anxieties about its future, it is important equally to focus on the structures of production and distribution which have underpinned the European film industry, and which, I suggest, directly reflect a similar conception of its function.

Louis Malle has been, from very early in his career, an 'independent' film-maker in every sense of the word. The box office success of his first film, *Ascenseur pour l'échafaud*, allowed him to buy out the production company Nouvelles Editions de Films, which has been involved in the financing of the majority of his films to date.[8] The further box-office success of *Les Amants* consolidated his financial autonomy, a factor which has allowed him considerable artistic autonomy; a freedom to choose which films he would make which is not often granted to film directors. In this respect he may be compared with Truffaut with his *Films du Carrosse*, and more recently, with Rohmer and his company, *Les Films du Losange*. This kind of small, independent, production company is typical of the European film industry, even if few directors enjoy the artistic freedom of Malle or Truffaut; and it stands in direct contrast to the dominant all-powerful studio system of the USA. Even when a project is co-financed with a television company, this pattern of small, ad hoc production remains, nonetheless, typical of the European industry. As I suggested earlier, this system of financing reflects, to a large degree, the free-wheeling independence of content of most European films. Malle himself, however, has refused to allow even this open and flexible structure to restrict him, and has made several films, usually those with large budgets, either in collaboration with the Hollywood studios or entirely financed by them. The list includes *Viva Maria* (1965), a mock-revolutionary Western starring Brigitte Bardot and Jeanne Moreau, set in the Mexico of Pancho Villa, and partly financed by United Artists; *Le Voleur* (*The Thief of Paris*, 1967), a costume drama about a gentleman thief, set in the *Belle Epoque*, also co-financed by United Artists; *Pretty Baby*, entirely produced by Paramount; *Crackers* (1983), a comedy-thriller and a disastrous flop produced by Universal and *Alamo Bay* (1985), a film about racism directed at Vietnamese

7. Ibid., p.66.
8. op.cit., French (1993), p.xiii.

immigrants, produced by Tri-star. It is typical of Louis Malle's career that, even when he worked in Hollywood, it was never with the same studio from one film to the next. Two of his most successful American films were not Hollywood productions at all: the intellectual conversation-piece, *My Dinner with André* (1981) was financed by its protagonists André Gregory and Wallace Shawn, and *Atlantic City* was mostly Canadian-financed, with some input from France. Clearly, the production patterns of Malle's films are as diverse as their themes and styles. One thing is constant, however, and that is the individualistic, improvisatory, and ad hoc approach to film production of Malle himself, which is certainly more typical of European production methods than American ones. Malle's position as a free-wheeling outsider in the American production system is thus mirrored by that of the protagonists in his films.

When it comes to his working methods as a director, Malle's style is nonetheless closer to that of the European art-house *auteur* than to that of the Hollywood craftsman, and this produced some characteristic difficulties during his period in America. In his European films, Malle was almost always involved in the writing of the screenplay, collaborating with figures as varied as Jean-Claude Carriére on *Viva Maria* and *Milou en mai*, the novelist Patrick Modiano on *Lacombe Lucien*, and the future director of *Cyrano de Bergerac*, Jean-Paul Rappeneau, for *Zazie dans le Métro*. In America, he found that his screen-writers were unaccustomed to working alongside the director in this way, and tended to produce independent, finished screenplays, without involving or consulting him[9]. In his shooting methods, he preferred to work in close collaboration with his European crew, but many of them (for example, his cameraman, Sven Nykvist), were unable to acquire permits to work with him in the United States[10]. In editing most of his films, he worked closely over twenty years with Suzanne Baron, and in this we can recognise the constitution of a regular team of technical collaborators which is typical of the approach of the European auteur. In casting his films, Malle regards the choice of actors as crucial to their success, and is equally capable of casting inexperienced non-professionals, such as Pierre Blaise in the title role of *Lacombe Lucien*, or of working with international stars at the peak of their fame, such as Brigitte Bardot and Jeanne Moreau in *Viva Maria*, or Burt Lancaster in *Atlantic City*. When he does use stars, they tend to be performers who have come to prominence in art-house films, rather than the typically commercial Hollywood icons. Whether working with non-professionals or stars, his direction seems to be very much actor-centred, involving a long process of careful preparation, rehearsal, and discussion with them[11]. In shooting, he is improvisatory in a way which is more European than American: he may shoot the same scene in several different ways, and from several different angles, so as to give himself a choice at the editing stage[12]. In the US this produced constant friction with the production-line methods of the American film crews, who were often irritated by his apparent uncertainty of purpose. In general, therefore, his working methods are recognisably those of the European rather than the American film-maker[13]. He tends to rely on a close collaboration with a carefully chosen team of actors and technicians, rather than on the anonymous skills of a studio crew. In this respect, his ability to empathise with the culture in which he is working, and his capacity for

9. Ibid., p.119.
10. Ibid., pp.119-120.
11. Ibid., pp.94-95.
12. op.cit., Mallecot (1977), p.64.
13. op.cit., French (1993), p.120.

close collaboration with a great variety of performers and technicians, must be seen as one of his distinctive strengths.

To attempt to draw a conclusion from this broad survey of Malle's work, it seems that even when he was working in America on profoundly American films such as *Pretty Baby*, *Atlantic City* or *Alamo Bay*, his working methods were nonetheless typical of the European director, with their characteristic emphasis on individual vision and directorial creativity, and at the same time their dependency on close collaboration with a hand-picked team of technicians and actors. The themes of his American films, with their provocative emphasis on amoral individualism, on marginality, and the refusal to conform to mainstream values, are essentially the same as those of his European films, and are also typical of European directors of the New Wave generation, such as Godard or Truffaut. His home-based French films, like *Lacombe Lucien* and *Milou en mai*, explore the roots of provincial, rural French culture in unusual and provocative ways, which suggest that for all the diversity of his output, he nonetheless gravitates towards a certain French national identity. A European film director, if one takes Louis Malle as a representative example, is likely to be grounded in a national culture, but not a prisoner of it; he is also likely to belong to a recognisable social class, as Louis Malle does, but not necessarily to identify with it. The films produced are likely to be marginal and individualistic, in relation to the dominant national culture, and to belong to an art-house film tradition of *auteurs*, rather than to the commercial mainstream dominated by Hollywood. European production methods are often ad hoc collaborations between individual production companies such as Malle's Nouvelles Editions de Films, and a range of other international co-production sources; most of Malle's output is made up of international co-productions. Extra finance for big-budget productions comes typically from Hollywood studios or European television companies, but there is no stable, pre-ordained system of production — this diversity is again reflected in the disparate output of Malle. In the end, a typical European film director is a marginal figure on the fringe of the society he works in, dependent on his wits and his talent to survive, often at odds with the social and commercial norms of European society as a whole, and with the American-dominated media. It is perhaps hardly surprising, in the light of this, that moral and ideological autonomy should emerge as such a fundamental theme in Louis Malle's own films.

Les Visiteurs: a popular form of cinema for Europe?

Anne Jackel

Science tells us that Homo Sapiens could laugh before they could talk, and Aristotle thought that laughter was a distinctive trait of humanity but, when it comes to appreciating twentieth-century art forms, *cinéphiles* tend to consider that comedy constitutes an inferior genre. However one of the earliest films was a comedy (*L'Arroseur arrosé*, Louis Lumière, 1895), and many of the greatest actors of silent cinema were comics, (for example, the actor-director Max Linder, 1883-1925), and plus two thirds of the box office successes of the last forty years have been comedies. Despite this the genre has been consistently snubbed by cinéphiles, neglected by historians and, more often than not, ignored by film critics.[1]

Today's cinema is more inclined to screen the early films of the Nouvelle Vague than some of the 150 films the French comic star Fernandel made between 1930 and 1970, or the greatest national box office hit of all times, *La Grande vadrouille* (*Don't look now, we're being shot at,* Gérard Oury, 1966) although this comedy, dealing with the French Resistance movement during the Second World War and starring Bourvil and Louis De Funès, remains one of the most popular films with television audiences in France.

With the exception of the works of writer-actor-director Jacques Tati, which have achieved something of a cult status, films that make people laugh are rarely shown at festivals, and seldom mentioned at award ceremonies, despite their popularity with cinema audiences. However, the extraordinary commercial success of *Les Visiteurs* (Jean-Marie Poiré, 1993), which achieved audience figures of over 13.5 million in France in 1993, may well have triggered a reappraisal of the genre, at least on the part of producers and financiers. If, worldwide, 1993 was the year of *Jurassic Park*, in France it was the year of *Les Visiteurs*, and this comedy has increasingly attracted the attention of sociologists, educationalists and historians alike.

In his book *Humour and History*, published the same year as the release of *Les Visiteurs*, Keith Cameron speculates that, 'if laughter is society's weapon to criticise departures from the norm, from the expected, to punish and to correct idiosyncrasies, then it should be possible to detect a relationship between the use of humour and the course of history'[2]. There is little doubt that, as far as the course of French cinema history is concerned, *Les Visiteurs* could not have appeared at a better time.

The 1980s saw a sharp decline in cinema attendance in France; the major reason being that the two most popular genres, comedies and thrillers, tended to be made for, or relegated to, the television screen rather than the cinema. The fall in the French share of the domestic market was such that, by the end of the decade, popular cinema seemed to be American rather than French, and the then Minister of Culture, Jack Lang, repeatedly expressed his fear that Cinema was in danger of disappearing before it reached its centenary. Subsequent measures were planned to change the

1. For example, it took ten years for one of the most popular makers of comedy, Claude Zidi, to receive a nomination for the French Awards ceremony, for *Les Ripoux* (The Cop, 1985). Moreover, in-depth analyses of particular aspects of comedy in *Les Cahiers du Cinéma* and other French critical journals, tend to focus on American Cinema.
2. Cameron, K. (ed.)(1993), *Humour and History*, Oxford: Intellect.

attribution of subsidies from the Automatic Support Fund, so as to penalize commercial films (equated to a great extent with large-budget films). However, this had little effect: Hollywood blockbusters continued to increase their share of the French market between 1987 and 1991, and the slight improvement occurring in 1992 was simply due to the entry in the French Top Ten of two French/English-language co-productions: *The Lover*, directed by Jean-Jacques Annaud, and *1492, Conquest of Paradise*, directed by Ridley Scott. 1993 marked a return to more protectionist policies, whether linguistic, in the wake of the language controversy surrounding the award of the Césars, the French equivalent of the Oscars, or financial, as illustrated by the measures adopted in summer 1993 by the new Minister of Culture, Jacques Toubon, to help the French film industry.

Despite reinforced government support in the last decade, one has to go back to 1985 to find a French film capable of attracting over 10 million people to French cinemas. The film in question, *Trois Hommes et un couffin* (*Three men and a cradle*) scripted and directed by a woman, Coline Serreau, was a light comedy dealing with men's changing role in child rearing. Two years later, the film was remade into the even more popular American *Three Men and a Baby*, whose world wide success was reflected by the production of a sequel, *Three Men and a Little Lady*. Coline Serreau's much acclaimed film constitutes a unique case in the 1980s, and ever since, French distributors have been lamenting the dearth of good, popular, French comedies on France's cinema screens.

In a cinematic climate favouring large-scale film budgets and sophisticated special effects, the huge success of Jean-Marie Poiré's modestly-priced comedy *Les Visiteurs*, costing a mere 60 million FF, took everybody by surprise. Co-produced by Gaumont and France 3 Cinema, the 100% French film received little attention from the critics at its release on 27 January 1993. However, within a month, the adventures of the twelfth century knight and his servant, magically transported into modern-day France, had become the most talked-about film of the season, and elements of the archaic vocabulary used by the two main protagonists even entered everyday slang. Winning over one million fans in its first two weeks, *Les Visiteurs* put French comedy once again at the top of the French box office ratings, and confirmed Jean-Marie Poiré's status as France's most inspired creator of comic cinema.

Of course, Poiré and his main actor and co-writer Christian Clavier were not new to commercial success, albeit on a smaller scale than that which greeted *Les Visiteurs*. The fifty-year-old French director has no pretentions other than being a popular filmmaker, whose aim is to produce films which will attract and please large audiences. As such, he rarely misses an opportunity to denounce what he perceives as the negative effects which the films of the French New Wave which he has always disliked, had had on the French film industry. The son of Gaumont producer Alain Poiré, he first came to public attention in 1981 with a *café-théâtre* style comedy entitled *Les Hommes préfèrent les grosses* roughly translated as 'Men Like Them Fat'. This fundamentally sexist film was scripted by Josiane Balasko, playwright, scriptwriter, and filmmaker, probably best known outside France for her role as Gérard Depardieu's plain secretary and mistress in Bertrand Blier's *Trop belle pour toi* (*Too Beautiful for You*, 1989).

Jean-Marie Poiré's next film, made the following year, the snappily paced and resolutely corrosive *Le Père Noël est une ordure* (*Father Christmas* is a Bastard) adapted from the SplendidTheatre play of the same title, and also starring some of the Splendid actors, including Josiane Balasko, Christian Clavier, Gérard Jugnot, Thierry Lhermite, has become a firm favourite with television viewers of all ages.

Since 1983, Jean-Marie Poiré has written exclusively with actor Christian Clavier. Together, they have developed a series of rich comedies, the most successful of which, at least until the release of *Les Visiteurs*, was *Papy fait de la résistance* (1983). A humorous story inspired by Jean-Pierre Melville's *Le Silence de la mer* (1948), it was itself an adaptation of a novel by Vercors, about a French family who are obliged to take in a German officer lodger, on the same day that they welcome a wounded British officer into their home.

Even allowing for the fact that parody is a natural feature of the genre, it is clear that innovation has never been a strong point of French comedy. In many ways *Les Visiteurs* is no exception; neither new (see *La Traversée de Paris*, 1956, starring Jean Gabin and Bourvil), nor typically French, the use of the male duo is a familiar theme in comedies in general, and even appearing a compulsory formula for the French comedies of the last decade. For instance, the Gérard Depardieu-Pierre Richard team achieved particular success with domestic audiences in films directed by Francis Veber: *La Chèvre* (*The Goat*, 1981), *Les Compères* (1983) and *Les Fugitifs* (1986).

Nevertheless, in other ways *Les Visiteurs* does break new ground as a comedy; for instance, it moves away from the tradition of 'niceness' which has been identified, by critics such as Françoise Audé, as a fundamental characteristic of French light comedies: 'Throughout the history of French cinema (even after 1968), French comedy has associated laughter with good naturedness. French comedy has respected its audiences 'taste for sweetness and light'[3].

Revolving around the somewhat facile and familiar contrasting of medieval customs and twentieth-century life, Poiré's comedy provides sharp observations about contemporary morals and characters, recalling for younger viewers *Back to the Future* and recognised by the French as referring to *François 1er*, a comedy made in 1937 by Christian Jaque, starring Fernandel In many ways, *Les Visiteurs* fits comfortably into Gerald Mast's category of the 'reductio ad absurdum comic plot', with a structure described by Mast as 'an investigation of the workings of a particular society, comparing the responses of one social group or class with those of another, contrasting people's different responses to the same stimuli, and similar responses to different stimuli'. Its plot too is typical of such comedies: 'multilevelled, containing two, three or even more parallel lines of action'. Quoting Renoir's *La Règle du jeu* (*The Rules of the Game*, 1939), and Clair's *A Nous la liberté* (1931), Mast suggests that there is something peculiarly French about this structure[4]. Whilst *Les Visiteurs* may well be reminiscent of the films of the 1930s in its cinematic structure, I shall argue later that such a structure is neither specific to the cinema or, indeed, typically French. Furthermore, a film based on class distinctions is a particularly rare occurrence in French post-war cinema. It seems wholly likely that

3. Françoise Audé, 'Gentillesse et complaisance dans la comédie française'. Paper presented to the *Conference on Popular European Cinema*, University of Warwick, September 1989.

4. Mast, G. (1973), *The Comic Mind: Comedy and the Movies*, New York: Bobbs-Merrill.

social theorists may, one day, choose *Les Visiteurs*, alongside such subversive comedies as Renoir's *Boudu sauvé des eaux* (*Boudu Saved From Drowning*, 1932), Faraldo's *Themroc* (1972), Blier's *Tenue de soirée* (*Evening Dress*, 1985), or Chatiliez's *La Vie est un long fleuve tranquille* (*Life is a Long Quiet River*, 1988), to provide illustrations of social differences.

It is interesting at this point to focus briefly on the last of these films: *La Vie est un long fleuve tranquille*. This is Etienne Chatiliez's first feature, from an original script which he wrote in conjunction with Florence Quentin. Based on an idea explored by Mark Twain in his 1894 novel *The Tragedy of Pudd'nhead Wilson*, the film tells the story of two babies who are swapped round by a nurse soon after birth. One comes from a respectable Catholic bourgeois family, the Le Quesnoys, the other from a plebeian, vulgar family of drop-outs and petty criminals from the other side of town, the Groseilles. *La Vie est un long fleuve tranquille* emerged as one of the greatest successes of the late 1980s, although its total box office receipts were only half those achieved by *Les Visiteurs*. It was frequently cited as a useful pedagogical tool in the study of class differences in Mitterrand's France. Curiously, five years later, the film critic of *Sight and Sound*, after remarking that 'dumping a medieval lord and his serf in present-day France allow[ed] for commentary on the foibles of bourgeois France in the 1990s', further suggested that *Les Visiteurs* might usefully be shown to British school children as a guide to the French class system, since 'it demonstrates better than most audio-visual aids that it is the lumpen-bourgeoisie who are the dominant class in France today and that the aristocracy is just a subculture among many'[5]. A characteristic France may well share with several of its European neighbours.

If neither film marks a decisive break with the established cultural and political ideology, both demonstrate a sense of irony verging on irreverence; both show that life is extremely funny, even if the humour relies heavily on overblown stereotypes[6]. In the case of *Les Visiteurs*, the social satire sends conflicting messages, in turn pleasing Right wing, Left wing, and Ecological Movements. As Keith Reader has noted, *Les Visiteurs* 'makes play with the Revolution (execrated by the scandalised knight, appreciated by his squire Jacquouille who elects to remain in the present day and enjoy its benefits), with the pretensions of the provincial bourgeoisie [...], and with the heritage industry (the knight's château transformed into a country hotel)'[7]. In both films, social order is disturbed but, in contrast with more conventional situation comedy, its hierarchies are not re-arranged and the return to the status quo is not unproblematic; factors which could in part account for the huge commercial success of these films, and for the reappraisal of *Les Visiteurs* by French intellectuals.

In an unprecedented move, the *Cahiers du Cinéma* critics, strong advocates of the Auteur theory, published, in March 1993, a six-page interview with Poiré and Clavier. In her introduction to the interview 'Les Visiteurs font de la résistance' (p.82), Camille Nevers stresses the importance of retaining a wide variety of film production, and quotes Marguerite Duras's claim that when a film starring Belmondo (one of the most popular stars of recent years) is a flop, the outlook for more intellectual and demanding films such as her own was increasingly poor.

To *Cahier*'s unexpected comments that, as a result of the French

5. *Sight and Sound*, vol. 4, no. 2, February 1993

6. Richard Dyer's suggests that the stereotype is commonly a device to 'maintain sharp boundary distinctions', between 'them' and 'us'. Marion Jordan argues that 'all fictional characters exist (at least in a limited sense) as stereotypes. This is to say no more than that the units of information about characters which we are given in fiction are necessarily larger and more discrete than the continuous elements of which actual people are constituted, since, contrary to artistic cant, it is art which is short and life which is long. [...] Without the use of synecdoche (whereby the part must be read as a whole) and metonymy (whereby a character is read from associated objects and surroundings), there can be no fictional recognition'. Jordan, M. (1983), 'Carry On...Follow that Stereotype', in Curran, J. and Porter, V. (eds.), (1983), *British Cinema History*, London: Weidenfeld & Nicolson.

7. Reader, K. (1994), 'L'exception culturelle: French Cinema Review of the Year', in *Modern and Contemporary France*, Vol. NS2, no.3.

Establishment's insistence on a cultural remit, and the marked preference of the CNC (Centre National de la Cinématographie, the French body responsible for the allocation of film subsidies), for cultural products with a high export potential, Berri's *Jean de Florette* (1986) and *Manon des sources* (1986), comedies such as *Les Visiteurs* had become increasingly difficult to make. Jean Marie Poiré adds that French actors must share the blame, in his experience, they often refused to appear in comedies, and when they reluctantly did agree to 'debase themselves' by doing so, they usually asked for a higher fee (p. 86).

In fact it is only thanks to the enthusiastic collaboration of the Splendid Theatre team that Poiré and Clavier were able to acquire their impressive reputation for lavish pictures which blend a wide variety of comic sources. Their films excel at parody and the subversion of standard genres, particularly French 1960s burlesque, and American slapstick comedy, and are notable particularly for their expression of Gallic humour. It is undoubtedly this quality, in combination with medieval knightly romance and amusing anachronisms, which ultimately accounts for the unprecedented box office success of *Les Visiteurs*.

It is important to recognise that *Les Visiteurs* belongs to a long French tradition of comedies anchored in national mythology. Poiré has claimed that he wrote a first draft of *Les Visiteurs* while he was still at school. Until relatively recently, the phrase 'nos ancêtres les Gaulois' (our ancestors the Gauls), was to be found on the first page of most French history text-books; a clear indication to schoolchildren that originally the French were, by definition, all Gauls. If, in recent years, relatively few films have explored the medieval patrimony, other forms of popular culture have successfully exploited the mass-appeal of this ancestral heritage. In recent decades, for example, the best-selling stories in print have been the *Asterix* series, selling more than 250 million copies since they were first published. Significantly, Euro-Disney's modest neighbour, Asterix Park, has been, relatively speaking, by far the more successful of the two.

As the authors of *Humour and History* remind us, deeply entrenched in Gallic medieval tradition is the very concept of 'l'esprit gaulois', a peculiar form of coarse humour, generally described as characteristic of, and destined for, the lower classes. In literature, such humour was already to be found in the medieval French 'fabliaux': short, comic, verse texts, whose subject matter was often concerned with the baser human instincts, and whose tone and language were crude, vulgar, realistic, and more often than not, downright rude.

The bawdy adventures of Godefroy de Montmirail and his squire Jacquouille-la-Fripouille bear many similarities to such ancestral texts, which claimed to have been written to entertain the common people. In formal terms, the numerous gags presented in rapid succession in *Les Visiteurs*, resemble the fabliaux-type short stories. Thematically, the travelling male duo was also a common trait of the genre and of the period. Linguistically, the valiant knight (Jean Reno) may be blessed with courtly speech, but his servant (Christian Clavier) uses a rejuvenated Old French language which owes much to the stylistics and the scatological witticisms of medieval literature in general, and to Gallic humour in particular.

Interestingly, this last concept has been challenged by the authors of

Humour and History, in their persuasive thesis that it is only during the last century that Gallic humour has become a national signifier. They pinpoint the moment at which it became accepted wisdom that 'l'esprit gaulois' was a particularly French phenomenon as the middle of the nineteenth century, 'a period when medieval literature, decent and indecent, was drawn on as source of national and nationalistic inspiration', and conclude from this that the supposed Gaulish lineage automatically led to the belief that 'l'esprit gaulois' was an inherent characteristic of French humour[8].

One can easily draw a parallel on the relationship between the appropriation of 'l'esprit gaulois' as national signifier and efforts to create a national consensus in nineteenth-century France with the public acclaim and subsequent critical reappraisal of *Les Visiteurs*, in a France struggling to preserve its cultural identity and a cinema driven by economic forces to redefine its identity in popular terms, on the eve of the twenty-first century. The fact that recent research has shown that such collective forms of appropriation of national aspirations belong to 'the imaginary' does not, however, make them less powerful[9]. Nor is such a phenomenon essentially French. Gallic humour may be particularly evident in the French 'fabliaux' but, as Trotter indicates, the medieval literary tradition 'lies at the heart of a pan-European tradition of bawdy comedy,' citing such examples as Chaucer and Boccaccio, the fourteenth-century German Gesamtabenteuer collection, and the goliardic verse of the Carmina Burana[10].

On the one hand, therefore, *Les Visiteurs*, drawing as it does on a common heritage of crude comic realism, can be regarded as a natural descendant of that European tradition, and on the other, Poiré and Clavier's frantically-paced comedy can also be read as a deliberate exercise in mixing more modern forms of humour: for exapmle, silent cinema gags, Monty Python one-liners, German scatological humour, and a parodic use of 'Franglais'. An approach stressing links with French literature, would draw attention to the obvious parallels between Béatrice Frénégonde de Pouille, the upper-class female character in *Les Visiteurs*, and the women targeted by Molière in *Les Précieuses ridicules*, whilst an Anglo-Saxon feminist approach could easily find a link between the Valérie Lemercier figure and Penelope Keith in *To The Manor Born*. The medieval backdrop and grotesque images of man's ineptitude provide a cultural framework made familiar to British viewers by such series as *Blackadder*, whilst a visual gag in *Les Visiteurs*, showing the knight staggering around after his head has been cut off, seems to have been directly lifted from Monty Python's *Holy Grail*. In other words, *Les Visiteurs* does not exclusively display a Gallic sense of humour, and indeed, the Gallic humour alluded to and overwhelmingly present in the film, does not constitute a cultural tradition that is unique to the French.

Poiré and Clavier, therefore, had good reasons for believing that, with its blend of traditional and contemporary comic genres, their film would enjoy as much success across Europe as it had at home. Along with the producer-director-actor team's hopes, the film also carried those of the French film industry, the CNC, the French Ministry of Culture, and the Board of Trade.

Furthermore, similar hopes have been expressed with regard to

8. Trotter, D. (1993), 'L'Esprit Gaulois, Humour and National Mythology', in Cameron, K. (ed.)(1993), *Humour and History*, Oxford: Intellect

9. Anderson, B. (1991), *Imagined Communities, Cahiers du Cinéma*, No. 465, March 1993, London: Verso.

10. op.cit., Trotter, D., 1993, p.76.

European cultural industries in general. A resolution drafted in the wake of the 1993 Symposium on 'The Future of European Cinema after the GATT Talks', states that 'European films must regain close contact with their audience'. Today, the latest Pan-European initiatives recommend a return to popular forms such as comedies, as a means of saving cinema. When asked, at the 1994 Felix award ceremony, about future developments at the European Film Academy, Aina Bellis, general secretary, replied that 'in the future, the Academy might introduce new categories to reach a more popular line-up, by splitting-up the main categories and having a comedy and/or family entertainment category'.

In medieval Europe, various 'treatises on medicine established a correlation between laughter and good health'[11]. Last December, the French Authorities appeared to have no qualms about the healing virtues of Les Visiteurs for the people of a France hit hard by the recession; even granting the film a special derogation to allow its early pre-Christmas release on video, instead of requiring the normal year's wait. However, thus far, Poiré's time-travel farce has proved a poor remedy for putting European cinema on the healthy road to recovery: in other European countries, the film has struggled to obtain even a tenth of its French success.

In countries where the film was subtitled, film critics and reviewers blamed its failure upon an extremely weak translation. It is undeniable that catch-phrases, clichés, aphorisms, and the Old-French dialogue used in Les Visiteurs at best suffered from translation into another language and, at worst, proved untranslatable (English subtitles such as 'Holy Scrotums' did not help). Nobody would disagree with Susan Purdie when she affirms: 'Joking emphasises the difficulty of translating any kind of utterance from one cultural context to another; and where the joke depends wholly upon one word form having multiple potential signifieds, the difficulty always entailed in translating from one tongue to another is manifest'[12]. Nevertheless, this point must not be exaggerated: Les Visiteurs uses a relatively small number of such utterances. Moreover, subtitles proved no obstacle to earlier French exportable products such as Mon Oncle (Jacques Tati, 1957), Cousin Cousine (Jean-Charles Tacchella, 1975), or Le Retour de Martin Guerre (The Return of Martin Guerre, Daniel Vigne, 1982). Les Visiteurs even shared with Vigne's film a medieval setting, with Cousin, Cousine, an explicit denunciation of the artificiality of relationships in contemporary bourgeois life, and with Mon Oncle, a caustic look at the modern world.

However, the two comedies, Mon Oncle, and Cousin, Cousine, included another two ingredients usually associated with French films: an auteur label, and sex; both of which are conspicuously missing from Les Visiteurs. British critical opinion found that Cousin, Cousine contained all the qualities that English audiences expected of a French film: it was sophisticated, adult, entertaining, and included the necessary romantic relationship. Unsophisticated, indeed intended as an antidote to the intellectual cinema which is the legacy of the French New Wave, neither strong on psychological subtleties nor particularly targeted towards an adult audience, Les Visiteurs therefore satisfied none of the expectations of foreign audiences as to what a French film should be. Even today, foreign audiences expect French films to be intellectual, or artistic; failing that, the (adult) high-brow audiences of art cinemas will enjoy large-budget historical

11. op cit., Cameron, K., 1993, p.5.
12. Purdie, S. (1993), Comedy, The Mastery of Discourse , London: Harvester-Wheatsheaf

melodramas or literary adaptations, whilst younger audiences prefer what Susan Hayward has called 'le cinéma du Look': *Diva* (Jean-Jacques Beneix, 1981), *Delicatessen* (Jeunet and Caro, 1992)[13]. In other words, if it is a comedy, the least they expect from a French director is a high comedy.

Few people in France doubted that the team behind *Les Visiteurs* had found the perfect recipe with which to refute the assumption that popular culture meant American culture, and that if there were a film capable of challenging the dominant opinion that French films were inevitably slow, boring, pretentious, parochial or intellectual, *Les Visiteurs* was the one.

Les Cahiers du Cinéma may have been prepared to renounce its elitist stance for the sake of the survival of a viable alternative to Hollywood, but distributors in Europe were more reluctant to put aside national stereotypes when it came to accepting this French film on their national screens. Outside France, therefore, audiences' expectations had a damaging effect on the reception of *Les Visiteurs*, and nowhere more than in Britain, where the film was subtitled and given a 15 certificate. Keith Reader astutely noted before its British release: 'not the least of [the film's] ironies is that a film pitched with overwhelming success at a mass audience will be confined in Britain to the very art-house public against which Christian Clavier has publicly inveighed — an interesting variation on the theme of inexportability'[14].

Where the film was released with subtitles, (as was the case in Britain), it flopped at the box office. Elsewhere, *Les Visiteurs*'s receipts never reached the levels of *Home Alone*, or *Mrs Doubtfire*, but there is enough evidence to show that, extensively promoted, the dubbed version of Poiré and Clavier's film could prove a crowd-pleaser with audiences as far apart, geographically and culturally, as Brazil and South East Asia. Even with the reputedly high-brow audiences of the French Film Festivals of Sarasota, Yokohama, Seoul and Tokyo, the success of the film was such that the producer-director-actor team received a standing ovation (to the great satisfaction of the French Minister of Culture or one of his representatives — usually present at those events which had been organized with the help of the French Film Export Agency, Unifrance). However, outside the Unifrance promotion circuit, *Les Visiteurs* was less well received on the whole. In Europe, audience reactions varied: it was popular in French-speaking regions of Belgium and Switzerland, and its dubbed version attracted over a million spectators in Spain, where it had been likened to Cervantes's *Don Quixote*, and where Spanish distributors had carefully selected commercial cinemas such as the Batista Soler Circuit in Madrid, given the film a 70-screen country-wide release, and allowed it to run for almost half a year. In Germany however, *Les Visiteurs*'s nine week screening managed 40,000 admissions, while in Britain, an eight-week run on the art-circuit hardly managed to draw 30,000 spectators.

The relative failure of the film outside its domestic market (and despite its obvious qualities) clearly illustrates that it will take more than a national box office hit, however huge it may be, to overcome the resistance of distributors, film critics, and audiences worldwide, and to persuade them that French/European films can be dubbed and that French/European dubbed comedies can cross national frontiers.

In February 1993, *Sight and Sound* predicted that it was highly unlikely

13. Hayward, S., (1987), 'France avance-détour-retour: French Cinema of the 1980s', in Howarth, J., (ed.), *Contemporary France*, London: Pinter

14. op.cit., Reader, K., 1994, p.308

that *Les Visiteurs* would enjoy international success because its references were so essentially French. I hope to have shown that its references, far from being peculiarly French, belong to a long established European tradition. One of the few values the film puts forward is ancestral continuity; surely likely to appeal to Europeans in search of roots for a new common identity?

Historians have recently argued that in the Middle Ages, the inhabitants of Europe were more European than they are today. The relative failure of a popular comedy to cross national borders in Europe may well prove them right. It certainly casts some doubts on the future prospects of a European popular cinema in a continent where, for many cinema-goers, the terms 'European' and 'popular' have become incompatible, or else thought to translate into the lowest common denominator. It also seems to undermine recent proposals, made at national and European levels, to support only those projects with a strong commercial appeal in order to take European cinema out of the limitations of the Art Circuit. It would be ironic if, in the aftermath of the GATT negotiations on cultural specificity, *Les Visiteurs*, when finally released in the United States in its dubbed version, were to be more successful there than it has been in Europe.

In Bergson's opinion, laughter is a tool with which society corrects aberrant behaviour. The French, laughing at and with *Les Visiteurs*, showed that they, at least, were prepared to recognise, if not quite to accept, the existence of aberrant behaviour. In 1988, Maillot argued that laughing at oneself requires a certain strength and robust self-awareness that has been missing from modern societies for a long time. In 1993, the French chose to be, in Mick Eaton's words, 'liberated by laughter'[15], but other critics and audiences showed nothing but contempt for a European alternative to the usual diet of American comedies. Perhaps the British film critic Iain Johnstone is right after all, when he asserts that, for most Europeans to-day, 'American humour is already in our veins, from the early silents to radio shows with people such as Jack Benny and George Burns and total television bombardment from *I Love Lucy*, to *The Golden Girls*[16].

With hindsight, the exemption made in the case of the 1993 pre-Christmas video release of *Les Visiteurs* in France may well be considered as a therapeutic measure whose short-term effects were guaranteed to rescue French citizens from the early symptoms of European melancholia and economic depression. In this respect, *Les Visiteurs* offered a timely solution to the former Minister of Culture's idealistic concern for the future of the art form of the twentieth century, and was also in line with the new Minister's endorsement of the more Cartesian message attributed to the French philosopher La Bruyère, that you should laugh before you are happy, because you may well die before you have a chance to laugh.

15. Eaton, M., (1981), 'Laughter in the Dark', in *Screen*, vol.22
16. Johnstone, I., (1993), 'You've got to be joking', in *The Sunday Times*, The Cultural Section 8, 29 December 1993

Wenders' *Paris, Texas* and the 'European way of seeing'

Stan Jones

In many ways, Wim Wenders provides a classic example of a self-conscious auteur. Following the release of *Alice in den Städten* (Alice in the Cities) in 1974, his films were crucial to defining the New German Cinema, and they remain central to any account of German film. By the mid-1980s Wenders claimed to have realised that it was essential for him, for reasons of personal identity, to decide upon his filmmaking identity: he opted for *European* [1]. By the time he felt the need to define himself in this way, Wenders had lived long enough in America to know he was never going to become an American. He had also found out, apparently through bitter experience, why he could never be an American filmmaker, that is, one able to work in the entertainment industry generally called 'Hollywood', described by him in an interview in *Der Spiegel*, as '...the modern Babel of Iniquity, the biggest racket you can imagine'[2]. His difficulties with Copolla on the production of Hammett (1982) are well-known, whilst his meditation on his German identity, in the series *Reden über Deutschland* (Talking about Germany) emphasises the importance to his public and private identities of his native language, describing his realisation that he was losing his personal identity as he found himself hesitating over using German, without the ability to compensate in American English[3]. Yet Wenders does not choose to define himself as a German filmmaker, and has committed himself to promoting European film through his chairmanship of the European Film Academy. Despite his extensive first-hand experience of the commercially and culturally dominant American industry, which constantly threatens the survival of the German or European production of films, he leaves open the question as to what a European film might be. Underlying his remarks, however, is the unspoken premise that such products would inevitably have to define themselves by contrast with the Hollywood model. He also warns of the supreme importance of retaining a specifically European cinema, since without its own images, Europe will lose its identity[4].

Although he sees the irony in his declared distrust of images and image-making when talking about his native country, Wenders's identity as a German filmmaker is undeniable; his company, Road Movies, operates out of Berlin, whilst the settings and iconography of his *Falsche Bewegung* (*Wrong Movement*, 1974), *Alice in den Städten* (*Alice in the Cities*, 1973), *Im Laufe der Zeit* (*Kings of the Road*, 1976), and latterly the Berlin 'legends': *Der Himmel über Berlin* (*Wings of Desire*, 1987) and *In weiter Ferne, so nah* (*Faraway, so Close*, 1993) illustrate German political and cultural history and, perhaps most importantly, the history of German cinema itself. But all the same, does it necessarily follow that Wenders the German filmmaker must be a European one? Beyond questions of iconography and intertextuality, what is it that could reinforce Wenders's own wish for European identity?

His *Paris, Texas* (1984) must be seen as pivotal, if for no other reason

1. Wenders, W., (1992), 'Nicht allein in einem grossen Haus' in W. Wenders, *The Act of Seeing*, Frankfurt/Main, Verlag der Autoren.
2. Wenders, W., (1987), interview in *Der Spiegel* 43, 19 November 1987, pp.230-238.
3. op.cit., Wenders, W., 1992, pp.187-197.
4. Wenders, W., (1993), 'Introduction from the Chairman of The European Film Academy' in Finney, A., *A Dose of Reality*, London: EMAP.

than that it follows his *Der Stand der Dinge* (*The State of Things*, 1983); a film which constructs an extended allegory about filmmaking as a reckoning with Wenders's own experience with the American industry. Its key scene comes when the director, Friedrich, asks his writer, a depressive called Dennis, why a Hollywood producer would want a European director. The writer responds with the ritual framing gesture and, with a degree of ironic self-stylisation, the two men formulate the answer between them: 'Die europäische Sehweise' (the European way of seeing). In *Paris, Texas* the European quality stands out although the film was shot in English in the American South-West with only minor German financing; and subsequently became the subject of a court-case over its release in the native country of its director.

As a product of 'the European way of seeing', this film was, and probably still is, the most widely successful that Wenders has directed, and has arguably contributed more than any of his other films to his reputation. The film's success certainly derives in part from its roots in genre conventions of narrative. In their recent study, Kolker and Beicken refer to Nicholas Ray's *Bigger than Life* to show how *Paris, Texas* combines the domestic melodrama with the western, above all through the parallels between Travis and Ethan Edwards from John Ford's *The Searchers*[5]. They also indicate the problematic nature of the references that *Paris, Texas* makes to American cinema and American culture, while drawing on both as the material for structuring its narrative. The way it uses these sources generates much of the film's tension between the narrative and the images. This in turn displays varying levels of allegorical potential, but without committing itself to any overall scheme of metaphorical reference — which is in itself an ironical position.

Such a potential multivalency is reflected in the range of critical responses to the film. In a brisk exchange in the German newspaper *Die Zeit*, following the release of *Paris, Texas*, Dieter Welleshoff dismissed the film as 'fromme Lügen' (pious lies) peddling a 'Trivialmythos' (trivial myth). More recently, Frieda Graf has commented on the overriding banality of Travis's story (Graf, 1972, p.9), whilst, on the other hand, Norbert Grob sees the film as a sort of enthusiastic ontology of the cinema, in which realities are transformed, and utopias made real[7], although it is difficult to see what utopian gloss *Paris, Texas* might bear.

In contrast to this interpretation is the more traditional understanding of 'the film's quite obvious sub-text of a Freudian-Oedipal conflict', in Mark Luprecht's identification of *Paris, Texas* as a tragedy[8]. Thomas Elsaesser and Timothy Corrigan have cited this film as marking a shift into postmodernity for Wenders's filmmaking, Elsaesser declaring that unlike Hollywood melodrama, *Paris, Texas* depicts a schizophrenic and unstable reality[9]. Corrigan, in his study of American cinema since Vietnam, deems Travis's journey an advanced stage of the road movie genre, in that it presents the spectacle of male narcissism[10]. From a similar American perspective, although without admitting any postmodern identity, Kolker and Beicken apply a similar conclusion allegorically to the wider culture: 'And even though Travis seems to have rid himself of his violent obsessions, he — like his namesake in *Taxi Driver* — drives into the night still full of threat in a culture that cultivates and supports men who are possessed by their desire to master women'[11].

5. Kolker, R. and Beicken, P. (1993), *The Films of Wim Wenders*, Cambridge and New York: Cambridge University Press.

6. Welleshoff, D., (1985), 'Fromme Lügen', in *Die Zeit*, 15 February 1985.

7. Grob, N., (1991), *Wenders*, Berlin, Edition Film

8. Luprecht, M., (1992), 'Freud at Paris, Texas: Penetrating the Oedipal sub-text', in *Literature and Film Quarterly*, no.2, 1993, pp.115-120

9. Elsaesser, T., (1986), 'American Graffiti und Neuer Deutscher Film - Filmemacher zwischen Avantgarde und postmoderne', in Huyssen, A. and Scherpe, K., *Postmoderne*, Hemburg, Rowohlt, pp.301-327.

10. Corrigan, T., (1991), *A Cinema without Walls*, New Brunswick: Rutgers University Press.

11. op.cit., Kolker, R. and Beicken, P.,1993, p.136.

All these interpretations depend on the mechanism of the narrative, to which Jochen Brunow refers in his collection, *Schreiben für den Film. Das Drehbuch als eine andere Art des Erzählens* (*Writing for the film. The shooting script as another sort of storytelling*). He puts his reservations about the film's narrative structure to Wenders himself, claiming that the film develops without ever finding itself, a point Wenders largely agrees with: 'Da mag Wahres dran sein. Die zweite Hälfte von *Paris, Texas* war ein totaler Blindflug. Und weil die erste so genau strukturiert war, merkt man das natürlich'[12]. (There may be some truth in that. The second half of *Paris, Texas* was a leap in the dark. And because the first half was so exactly structured, you notice that, of course.)

Wenders insists that there is a clear direction throughout the narrative, thus allowing the possibility of what we might identify as an allegorical function. This derives from and illustrates the 'European way of seeing' in Wenders's work, and shapes this film through its development of what might well be seen as the dominant concern of his entire opus: the theme of seeing, viewing and spectatorship[13]. The film's narrative requires its characters to be both observers and players; Travis, for example, switches from the role of observer to that of central player, then back to observer, before quitting the action he has initiated. Jane and Hunter exhibit the same duality, but it proves beyond the capability of Walt and Ann, who must therefore be excluded from the narrative.

As the film is a product intended for watching, the audience too must take on the two roles; a situation with an implicit irony in the sense of Jean-Louis Comolli's observation: 'Never passive, a spectator works. But that work is not only a work of decipherment, reading, elaboration of signs. It is first of all and just as much, if not more, to play the game, to fool him or herself out of pleasure, and in spite of those knowledges which reinforce his or her position of non-fool'[14].

Wenders constantly reminds us that we are playing the game of spectators of a fictional process; a process, moreover, that functions through the manipulation of our sense of time, sometimes even revealing something to us about that very sense.

Although *Paris, Texas* contains no effect that might alienate us outright, it does require from us a particular version of the ironic stance implied in Commolli's description. Self-conscious references to spectating dominate the film at all levels: the initial bird's eye view of Travis; the shots of Walt, the brother who rescues him, framed against his advertising posters; the repeated shots in close-up of still photographs; the elaborate film-within-a-film in the home-movie sequence; the manipulation of the mirror in the chat-house; the final view of Travis in his driving mirror. All these references, of course, recall Wenders's belief that, for him, the camera functions always in two directions: showing its viewing subjects just as much as its viewed objects[15], and this ironic, self-conscious stance must be recognised as part of Wenders's essentially European way of seeing.

In the opening sequence, we look directly down on Travis who, significantly, appears to be aware that he is being watched. In other words, we, the spectators, figure in our own first sight of the hero. A little later, Walt indirectly draws us into the three-dimensionality of the scene in which he urges Travis to leave the railway track he is following. As Walt

12. Brunow, J., (ed.)(1991), *Schreiben für den Film: Das Drehbuch als eine andere Art des Erzählens*, Berlin, Edition Text und Kritik.
13. Visarius, K., (1972), 'Das Versagen der Sprache oder: His Master's Voice' in Jansen P.W. and Schütte, W. (eds.), *Wim Wenders*, pp.43-64, Munich: Hanser.
14. Commollo, J-L., (1990), 'Machines of the Visible', quoted in H. Schlüpmann, 'Schulust und Ästhetik', in Hickethier, K. and Winkler, H., (eds.)(1990), *Filmwahrnehmung*, Berlin: Sigma Bohn.
15. op.cit., Jansen, P.W. and Schütte, W., 1972, p.101.

insists that 'there's nothin' out there', we are given a protracted view, from the characters' perspective if not through their eyes, of the famous illusion of parallel lines meeting at infinity. There is a particular irony in the sight of one character in a film inviting another to acknowledge the emptiness of one of the film's images, through a basic demonstration of cinema's most fundamental illusion of three-dimensionality. Just as Travis has to play the game of acknowledging his brother's common-sense view, thereby beginning to re-integrate himself into his brother's normality, so too we have to acknowledge the image as part of the narrative of this re-integration, and to play the game as the film audience.

The final stage of the process of reintegration occurs in Walt's house when Travis' family history is revealed in the form of a home-movie. Wenders's presentation of this sequence, which leads to the reconciliation of father and son, and of the family group as spectators of the film, is melodramatic. However, we the spectators of the 'real' film, are denied any such melodramatic viewpoint, thus complicating the relation between the home-movie and its narrative function.

At this point, Travis experiences, in a fragmentary form, proof of the authenticity of an element of his past, whose memory he has just disavowed. He sees himself as a player in the events, and must therefore have been an observer of them at the time. But more than that, he must also have been one of the player/obervers who created the record. The images follow a natural chronology, despite Walt's mention of their having been strung together. The home-movie is not structured according to the conventions of film fiction, or even of documentary, and represents no more than a record of existence. As video now has taken over the function of domestic recording, the film format appears anachronistic, a further reminder that we are viewers of a medium that by its very form can only be regarded as representing reality in the past. If it has any reality in the present, it is in the reactions of the viewers to it, and above all in their willingness to play the game as viewers. With surprising rapidity, for him, Wenders intercuts between the film and its reception, to show Travis' reaction, and his exchange of looks and comments with Hunter. At one point he manipulates our viewpoint in a particularly melodramatic manner by directing us back to Travis through rack-focus shifting within the shot. The shared experience of the film unites father and son so that the narrative can now shift forward, allowing them to become players in their joint narrative present.

As viewers, we are faced with ambiguous and shifting accounts. As we watch the home-movie sequence, we see Jane (Travis' wife) spreading a scarf over the lens of the camera which Travis was using to film her, but we also see that Travis now finds it unbearable to look at that sequence. He wants to avoid both the projected image of Jane, and the visible evidence of his own participation in creating that image. However, our viewings of the home-movie do not share the viewpoint of any of the household. To us, it appears fullscreen, whilst the musical soundtrack of *Paris, Texas* cuts in simultaneously with the projector noise. So we are with them in their viewing, but also subject to the manipulation of whatever consciousness exposes us to the music as adjunct to the images. We are at the same time viewers in a cinema, who happen to be watching a home-movie in all its grainy authenticity, and members of the group of fictional characters whose very existence depends on our being willing to believe that, for them, these images represent authentic history. We are, in other words, simultaneously involved and held at an ironic distance[16].

We, the cinema audience, have to renounce any detached viewing position when we share with the film's domestic audience the experience of Walt gesturing to a third party, who has managed to get them all into shot, as he reclaims the camera. He reaches out of the bottom of the frame and in so doing visually disorientates us by the sort of naive manipulation of our point-of-view that signals the 'amateur' product. By showing us his character Walt effectively taking his own camera back from us, Wenders challenges us to 'play the game'. If we want the story to continue, we too, like Wenders's characters, must act as player/observers by accepting the historical reason for this manoeuvre, which serves visually to reinforce the characters' memories of being players in the action their film records.

The family photos that Travis and Hunter examine together fulfil the same function, and their shared pleasure in their reactions to them confirms their relationship. Ironically, this takes place in the home built by billboards, the sort of images we see Walt actually dismantling and re-constructing as Travis comes to tell him of his decision to find Jane. The constructed hoarding shows a clichéd soft porn image, providing us with an ironic preparation for Travis's initial reaction to the image of Jane in the peepshow. And given the outcome of their meeting, it is ironic in retrospect that Travis, who apparently likes billboards, can only see clearly from the gantry because his back is turned to the image being created behind him.

Walt, despite all his solid reasonableness and genuine affection, must ultimately relinquish his role as father because he creates such images for a living. What enables him and Ann, according to the film's narrative logic, to care for Hunter practically, may also indicate, in the film's scheme of allegorical images, the main reason why they must lose him. In this respect our first sight of Walt constitutes a signal: it is a piece of *trompe-l'oeil* as he talks into his mobile phone in front of the two-dimensional image of a skyscraper: a strangely flat image inserted into a film dominated until then by a huge depth of perspective.

In his relationship with Hunter, as most studies on *Paris, Texas* indicate, Travis gradually seems to assume a paternal role. This begins with their joint viewing of photographs, and culminates with Travis's final explanation of the picture of the vacant lot in Paris, Texas. Hunter refuses to read Travis's dream of a family home into the photograph, and thus refuses to play the game as observer of the site where his father would have a role for him as a player. The film does not manipulate our point-of-view here; Travis abandons his delusions along with the image on which they had been focused. The fictionality of the characters is therefore not at risk, and the film treads a very fine line between providing, and subverting, a straight melodramatic narrative.

It is this scene that can set the narrative in motion once again after it has stopped dead with the image of Jane that Travis has to confront at the chat-house. Wenders shifts us between Travis's viewpoint through the one-way glass, with a close-up of him from the side, and the near reverse angle to show Jane looking at her own reflection. This shifting creates the *mise en scène* which demonstrates, through the peepshow mirror, the narrative

16. op.cit., Elsaesser, T., 1986, p.305.

logic for the resurgence of Travis's obsessive jealousy: Jane is an image for
hire, one which offers an unknown man the privilege of observing without
being observed, the classic voyeur viewpoint. As an observer, Travis is in a
situation analogous to viewing a film, and simultaneously we, of course,
are watching him watch. However, the intercom system enables him to
alter the woman's image by communicating with her. Since he does not
ask her to change her image in any way, she takes the initiative and offers
to be a listener for him. This offer provokes his flight, since it would cause
him to reveal his identity, and would rob him of the advantage of the
mirror. However, we do not leave with him. Instead, the narrative stops
dead, and we remain behind while, disturbingly, a character in a film looks
directly at us, without any overt irony, inviting us to communicate with
her. We know this is possible from the *mise en scène* we have observed, but
we also know that it is totally impossible within the process of film-viewing.
Paris, Texas here issues its most direct challenge to us to carry on playing
the game, and it reinforces our disorientation by shifting into slightly
greater close-up. Just as Travis cannot communicate, neither can we, and
Wenders reinforces this point by cutting back, as it were, behind the screen,
to show his character's disquiet at the inevitable lack of response from the
other side. However, once there, we have returned to our privileged
position vis-à-vis the film character, and so the narrative can continue.

At the second meeting, Jane recognises Travis' voice, and her attempt
to see through the mirror turns it into a partial mirror in the opposite
direction. Her image looks out at us again, but as we have been shown
Travis with his back to her telling his story, the narrative motivation prevents
the image from disorientating us. Travis then turns his chair back to the
mirror, and in so doing, creates what must be the central image of *Paris,
Texas*, and certainly one of the most frequently quoted. There is no doubt
of the symbolic effect of the superimposition of Travis' image upon that
of Jane. The effect is clearly reinforced when he declares: 'I can't see you,
Jane', as they try to make the mirror transparent, by altering the lighting
on either side of it. Jane too has to turn away from what she can see of
Travis, before she can tell her story. Unlike Travis, however, she relates it to
the present circumstance by telling it in the first person, starting from the
time of their separation, whereas he distances himself from his own history,
by telling it in the third person, almost as if it were a parable about
individuals who might be anyone at all.

There will be no reconciliation, because the pair fail to deconstruct
the cinematic circumstances of their meeting. A commonsense approach
to the plot might ask why they are unable to meet when Travis first goes
up the backstairs to the bar of the club. Were Travis not driven out from
the bar at that point, the actual situation of the meeting would be secondary
and would correspond to the codes of melodrama. These, in turn, would
dictate the significance of any resolution. Such a reliance on established
forms would inevitably reduce the tension between images and narrative
in the film, so that the meeting would function in a way that recalls the
celebrated scene from Nicholas Ray's western *Johnny Guitar*[17]; as hero
Johnny and heroine Vienna find each other again, the narrative motif of
lovers reunited requires them to decide how they will reconstruct their
joint history, with all its implications for gender roles. Before they can

17. The scene is quoted by
Almodóvar in his *Women
on the Edge of a Nervous
Breakdown*.

resume their relationship, the pain of their past involvements is expressed through the manufacture of mutually acknowledged lies about how much they have missed each other. This device subverts the love story melodrama, as Vienna concurs with Johnny's wishes, and reinforces his bitterness and jealousy over their mutual past, before making him aware of her own distress. Yet we the viewers are then asked to accept that she is so infatuated with him that she will, after all, join him in dismissing the past hurt as a dream and construct a mutual self-deception about their relationship even to the extent of accepting his offer of marriage, of all-embracing domesticity. We have to assent to the shifting of the narrative back into standard melodrama, so that a happy ending can be provided.

Ray's film offers the assurance that there is a storyteller in control of its narrative, so that we can expect a satisfactory resolution of its myth. By contrast, the meetings of the ex-lovers in *Paris, Texas*, show us a process in which each creates a position from which to act as spectator, observing himself or herself. In that Jane speaks as 'I' to 'you', she goes further than Travis in overcoming the barrier separating them, but she still has finally to admit that she cannot recover the sense of his separate, individual identity. Travis is irrevocably stuck in the cinematic situation because he can only tell his story as if he were watching someone else. Both characters are incapable of becoming players once again in a domestic/family situation.

Wenders's film shows us the telling of the two stories, but it does not use flashback to show us the stories, even though Travis's account would lend itself to that treatment. However, were he to show the story visually, he would turn the film into a melodrama, because it would provide for its spectators a version of past events which would define our reactions to what we see as the film's present, and would therefore imply an inherent moral or ethical verdict on the circumstances and the people in them. This, in turn, would suggest that there is a proper or correct position for the viewer, decided in advance by the filmmakers, and would imply that somewhere just over our shoulders, as we sit in the dark watching the images, there is a storyteller who not only knows what happened, but also shows us what we need to know in order to evaluate what we see. Inevitably, this would suggest that there is only one correct reading of the film; a spectator position which conforms to a universally acceptable definition of the ideology underlying cinematic melodrama, and dominates the mainstream Hollywood film[18].

In *Paris, Texas*, however, the storytelling sequence leaves us with the unoccupied mirror as an indication that there will be no further development of this couple's story. The narrative pace may pick up again, but it does not produce any closure; by now the story is all over, and the characters themselves have realised that.

Does *Paris, Texas* therefore leave us with the bleak prospect of no underlying myth? On the most superficial level, the film could perhaps be seen as a warning about the dangers of trying to force others to conform to your image of them. Elsaesser extends this point to consider the close of *Paris, Texas* as providing an ironic 'solution' to Wenders's abiding theme of the difficulty of men's relationships with women, all done via 'a story in which the protagonists make each other into mere signs, deprive each other of reality and become figures of their anxieties and wishes'[19].

18. The conditioned viewpoint can be demonstrated by draawing a contrast with Wender's own work. A scene from *Der Himmel Über Berlin* (*Wings Of Desire*) shows one of his recording angels, Damiel, indulging his fascination for Marion, the trapeze artist of a small circus, by watching her through the back of her dressing-mirror as she meditates on her sadness over the circus closing. Marion looks directly at us, straight at the camera, in other words; however, our somewhat detached viewpoint presents us with a romantic melodrama, and is very different from the insecure and occasionally disorientating position we occupy in Paris, Texas.

19. op.cit., Elsaesser, T., 1986, p.325

Against this, Luprecht's discovery of the Oedipal sub-text (see page 102) which, he claims, is there without Wenders knowledge[20], suggests Travis and Jane both manage to reconstitute their personalities. By recognising in himself the transmission of his father's fault, Travis might thus attain a certain tragic greatness, by restricting himself to the role of observer, he denies himself that of player, or father who may pass on the fault to his son. Corrigan's final interpretation would deny us, the audience, any such satisfactory myth, by indicating how the Travis who stands finally in the parking lot outside the hotel has constructed for himself a position in which he can be both father and son, lover and child.

As it can carry this range of interpretations, Wenders's film functions as an allegorical narrative that denies any final revelation, any assurance for its audience of knowledge to be gained from it. Its significance and its value, and perhaps, ultimately, the mark of its 'European way of seeing', lie in its inherent and shifting tensions: it operates with the paradox of demonstrating to its viewers the dangers of involvement with the mythologising process of cinema, whilst all the time itself exploiting cinema's capacity to persuade us that its stories reflect our situation, even if only at second-hand, through reference to our experience of 'playing the game' in classic melodramatic narratives, and that they deserve our attention just as much as anything we consider relevant to our lives. In this way, the film can be seen as an attempt to use a European way of seeing via imagery taken from America, the source of the great competitor industry, to ensure the audience's ability and willingness to play its role as viewers, but in a game whose rules are ultimately European[21].

20. op.cit., Luprecht, M., 1992, p.120.
21. Here Andrew Higson's concluding remark to his essay on 'The Concept of National Cinema' is pertinent: '...the question of audiences has to be crucial for the study of national cinemas. For what is a national cinema if it doesn't have a national audience?' Higson, A., (1989), 'The Concept of a National Cinema', in *Screen* vol. 30, no. 4, pp. 36–46.

Identity and the past in recent Russian cinema

David Gillespie

Cinema in post-glasnost Russia, like every other field of cultural endeavour, has undergone a profound and probably irreversible revolution. With the disappearance of the old certainties, across the countries of Eastern Europe nationalism fills the gap left by the collapse of ideology. It would, however, be wrong to assume that the emerging search for national self-consciousness is a new phenomenon. In Soviet cinema, as in literature, the search for new forms of expression and new ideas of belonging and destiny began with the death of Stalin in 1953, and assumed certain shapes in the 1960s. Particularly since the 1960s, writers and film-makers in Russia and the USSR have turned their attention to the historical past, in an attempt to find out the truth, and also to reflect on the events and personalities that have shaped the present. This chapter will examine some films of the post-Stalin period that deal with the past, in an attempt to give a picture of the emerging ideas of national self-awareness and the historical destiny of Russia.

Before looking at films, however, it is necessary to discuss ideology. For decades, socialist realism was the only acceptable artistic method in Soviet culture, and this method applied equally to music, art, cinema, literature, and even architecture. Socialist realism basically required the artist to show how all conflicts can be resolved with the aid of the Party, and that the future was being built according to the wise doctrine of the Party. In practice it meant that anything that suggested that the Party was not in control, or worse, that it was corrupt, or that actual situations did not conform to their ideological projections, was deemed unacceptable. In cinema, the screenplay was thus of vital importance, as it was the main means of conveying the propagandistic method. The screenplay would be completed before filming, having been supervised by the Party, and could not subsequently be developed or changed without Party permission. The finished product would then be viewed by Party and film officials[1]. Films which were deemed unsuitable, for whatever reason, were put on the shelf and not made available to the public. Thus in cinema, as in literature, the years 1986–88 largely saw the release of films that had been on the shelf, perhaps for up to twenty years.

The supervision of the cinema industry was carried out by Goskino, the committee with sole responsibility to finance and distribute films. Goskino also had the power to prevent films from being shown if they did not conform. The persecution of Andrei Tarkovskii in the 1970s and 1980s is ample evidence of the abilities of this organization to enforce its will on Soviet film-makers. That is, he was allowed to make films, but these films were given only a restricted showing, if at all, and Goskino even argued against the award of prizes to Tarkovskii at major international festivals[2].

Socialist realism also promulgated the idea of the socialist fraternity, the coming together of all peoples under the Soviet banner of

1. Kenez, P. (1992), *Cinema and Soviet Society, 1917-1953*, pp.101–185
2. Tarkovskii, A. (1991), *Time within Time: The Diaries 1970-1986*, translated by Kitty Hunter-Blair, Calcutta, Seagull

internationalism. Individual nationhood was therefore subordinated to the idea of the greater Soviet 'family'. The opening of the floodgates in 1986–87, not surprisingly, saw a release of pent-up anger, frustration, and bile, that has done much to shape the emerging social and civic consciousness in the Russian cinema. One of the major themes, not surprisingly, in these years, has been the sense of historical injustice, especially crimes committed in the name of the Party under Stalin. The age-old Russian questions are asked: how did this happen? Who is to blame? What are we to do now? What does the future hold? Such questions are at the root of such seemingly divergent subjects as the problems of youth, the investigation of the past, and the soap-opera-like pictures of spiritual and moral conflicts set in a recognizably drab and desolate urban present.

It is instructive at this point to look at the example of literature, as its links with cinema will become increasingly obvious. Certainly, observers of the literary scene in Russia over the last thirty years have commented on the emergence of several groups professing to 'rediscover' Russia, its literature, and its cultural identity. These groups, originating in the mid-1960s, have usually been based around literary journals such as *Young Guard* and *Our Contemporary*, and now not only affirm the greatness and uniqueness of Russian literature, but also espouse hardline attitudes towards other nations (especially the West), strong autocratic leadership, and an accompanying contempt for democracy and parliamentarianism. There are heated arguments between so-called 'patriots' and 'democrats' on what Russian literature is, and what makes a Russian writer. Russian nationalist writers and critics of varying hues attempt to define a particularly 'Russian' literature, excluding from its canon such established and respected authors as the Jewish Isaak Babel', Osip Mandel'shtam, and even Boris Pasternak, or the Kirghiz Chingiz Aitmatov. The search for national identity has taken place not only in the critical press, but also in fiction, especially in the works of the so-called 'village writers': Vasilii Belov, Vladimir Soloukhin, Boris Mozhaev, Viktor Astaf'ev and Valentin Rasputin are the main representatives of this trend still alive, representing a range of nationalist viewpoints[3].

There is a clear link between 'village prose' and nationalism in film, for some of the major successes of 'village prose' were made into equally (if not more) successful films: Elem Klimov's 1983 film *Farewell*, an adaptation of Rasputin's 1976 novella *Farewell to Matera*, and Vasilii Shukshin's 1973 novella *Snowball Berry Red*, written especially for the cinema, which Shukshin not only directed himself, but in which he also played the leading role, are two outstanding examples. In *Farewell*, a three-hundred-year-old island community on the river Angara in Siberia is threatened with destruction as a hydro-electric dam is built upriver. The dam requires a huge reservoir, of which the river will form part, and, as the water level is to be raised, the village Matera is to be flooded, its culture, traditions and history consigned to oblivion. Both the author of the original novella, Rasputin, and the film- maker, Klimov, invest the story-line with considerable lyricism and symbolism, to create an elegy not only for a disappearing rural way of life, but also as a statement on the fate of Russia in the industrial age. There is also considerable anger at the way in which

3. For information on the 'new right' and nationalism, I am indebted to Kathleen Parthé, in particular her paper 'The Empire Strikes Back: How Right-Wing Nationalists Tried to Recapture Russian Literature', presented at the *26th Annual Convention of the American Association for the Advancement of Slavik Studies*, Philadelphia, November 1994.

decisions are taken, thousands of miles away in Moscow, that affect the lives of people whose views are not even sought. In the novella, the bureaucracy, and the so-called 'sanitary engineers' who come to 'cleanse' the island of its trees and houses (so that they do not protrude above the water level after the flooding), are seen in negative, inhuman terms, outsiders destroying the homes of others; in the film, their depiction is ambivalent, as they are seen as 'necessary'. Both film and novella nevertheless offer an apocalyptic picture, as Matera is to be razed by fire before being flooded by the rising waters of the dam. Consequently, man's link with the land, and his cherished link with the past and with his ancestors, is lost[4].

In *Snowball Berry Red*, we are introduced to Egor Prokudin, a thief and ex-con, on his release from prison. Failing to be accepted back into his former gang, he becomes disillusioned, and attempts instead to get a job on a farm and settle down. He goes to live in a village near where he was born. Prokudin, it transpires, was separated from his parents while a teenager; one of the millions of Russians uprooted and torn from their rural origins through Stalin's disastrous policy of collectivization in the late 1920s. Just as Prokudin appears at last to have found his place — as a tractor driver, symbolically re-establishing his links with the land — his gang come to reclaim him as one of their own, and in the ensuing fight, Prokudin is killed. The film asserts the moral superiority of the village over the town, where the village is populated by essentially good and wholesome folk, and danger lurks only when it is threatened by outsiders. The town, on the other hand, is the home of criminals, and a place of debauchery. Undeniably a powerful and compelling film, *Snowball Berry Red* was phenomenally popular in Russia in the 1970s exactly because millions of ordinary Russians, similarly uprooted and alienated, identified with it. Tarkovskii revealed that his film *Mirror* (1975) was similarly received, as the lives and experiences of millions are reflected through the destiny of an individual.

More fundamentally, in both films (as well as the literary works on which they are based), urban lifestyles are consistently contrasted with the lives of simple people from the village. The village and the countryside are more wholesome, morally pure, than the city; people from the city have sold their souls in exchange for spurious material benefits. Moreover, the village is the repository of age-old customs and values, it is where the national character itself is rooted. In short, the village is Russia, and the move to urbanization leads to disaster. In the village prose movement, and the films that proceeded from it, there is the affirmation of a mythical picture of Russia, a Russia whose heritage lies in the countryside, and where corruption, and ultimately death, accompany urban ways and industrialization.

Yet compare this to Andrei Mikhalkov-Konchalovskii's *Asya's Happiness* (1967), a simple and unadorned picture of collective farmers gathering in the harvest during a palpably hot and sweaty summer, and the private life of the Asya of the title. In this film there is no idealization of rural life or the rock-solid values that purportedly emerge from it. Furthermore, there is no cinematic stylization: there is little background music, the action is filmed almost in a documentary, fly-on-the-wall fashion, and there are few professional actors. The director allows his villagers to speak in their

4. Parthé, K. (1992), *Russian Village Prose: The Radiant Past*, Princeton University Press.

natural idiom, retelling stories of the War and the Stalinist purges in a natural and straightforward way, without any sensationalism or sentimentality. The overall effect of the film is to give a picture of a strongly bonded community whose members share the same faith, beliefs, and outlook on life, and expect little from life other than what they receive through the fruits of their labour. They are at one with their environment (as the camerawork stresses, catching individuals against the backdrop of fields, river and rolling hills). It is a raw and unadorned picture of ordinary people at work, and relaxing, speaking about their own lives, in their own language, and consciously rejecting any nationalist or so-called 'patriotic' uplifting interpretation of Russia's hardships. It is perhaps exactly because of the absence of any ideological underpinning that this film was withdrawn from circulation in the USSR for twenty years.

I think that the films of Andrei Tarkovskii, perhaps the best-known Russian film-maker of his generation, are also relevant here. In such films as *Nostalgia* (1983), and *Sacrifice* (1986), both made in the West, he, too, reflects on Russia's national identity, in the form of its relationship with the West. Whereas in earlier films made in the Soviet Union, such as *Andrei Rublev* (1965), and *Mirror* (1974), Tarkovskii had pondered this relationship and found scope for cooperation and accommodation between Russia and the West, when he actually arrives and works in the West, he rejects any communication. In true Slavophile tradition, a homesick and despondent Tarkovskii saw the West as morally bankrupt, devoid of spirituality, and heading for catastrophe. In *Nostalgia* he rejects the idea of mutual understanding, as he, the *auteur*, tries to transform an Italian landscape into something resembling Russia, just as Gorchakov, the erstwhile hero, tries to see Russia all around him. Thus, he sees a mad Italian hermit as a Russian 'holy fool' foretelling the end of the world, and finds it impossible to achieve any real communication with his beautiful Italian guide. She, in particular, is made to look superficial, a Russian speaker who cannot penetrate beyond the surface meaning of the words in the poems she reads (significantly, poems written by Tarkovskii's own father). The end of the film sees the gradual merging of a Russian and Italian landscape, with Russian folk music blending with Verdi's *Requiem* in the background. External landscapes are confused, juxtaposed, but inner, psychological landscapes remain distinct, separate. In *Sacrifice* Tarkovskii's predicted catastrophe happens, as nothing less than nuclear war is the theme[5].

In this context it is instructive to turn to a documentary film, *The Russia We Have Lost* (1992), by Stanislav Govorukhin. This film offers a kind of socialist realism in reverse, where the Tsarist past and, in particular, the Tsarist family, are presented in glowing colours, with hardly a mention of the repression, poverty, institutionalized anti-semitism or chronic civil backwardness historians tell us were prevalent. The destruction of the monarchy is said to have been an unmitigated catastrophe for Russia. Furthermore, the director, who also narrates and presents the film, is intent to impress upon the viewer not only a nostalgic and rose-tinted picture of Russia as a nation with a glorious heritage, but also as a great power. Throughout the film the point of reference is 1913, the year before the outbreak of the First World War, which led to the abdication of the Tsar

5. I have written at more length on Tarkovskii's Slavophilism in my paper 'Russia and the West in the films of Andrey Tarkovsky', *New Zealand Slavonic Journal*, 1993, pp. 49-61.

and the Bolshevik seizure of power in 1917. Although Govorukhin admits the weakness of the Tsar, he is enamoured of the pageantry and majesty of the royal family, its links with European monarchs, and spares us no details in his blow-by-blow account of the brutal murder and disposal of the bodies of the entire Romanov family in 1918.

Significantly, the major circumstance that destroyed the credibility and legitimacy of the Romanov dynasty — the influence of Grigorii Rasputin at court in the last years of the monarchy — is totally ignored in this film.

Govorukhin is at pains to paint a black picture of Lenin as a cynical opportunist with a pathological hatred of the monarchy, and also spends considerable time exploring Lenin's Jewish ancestry. All in all, the glorification of the Tsarist past is not that far removed from the idealization of a mythic Russia in the films by Klimov and Shukshin, and it is not surprising, therefore, that in the closing credits Govorukhin acknowledges in particular his debt to the writings of Alexander Solzhenitsyn.

Solzhenitsyn, too, has much in common with the 'village prose' movement — indeed, with his novella *Matryona's Home* in 1963, he started it — but the film *The Russia We Have Lost* (1992) follows exactly Solzhenitsyn's interpretation of Russian history in the early years of this century, including his advocacy of Stolypin, the reformist Tsarist minister whose efforts to modernize agriculture and the rural community are seen by Solzhenitsyn as offering the way forward for Russia in the years before the First World War. Stolypin was assassinated in 1911, and with him, according to the Solzhenitsyn variant, went Russia's chances of averting revolution and catastrophe.

A word perhaps could be added here on another film by Klimov, *Agony*, released only in 1985, about the last days of the Romanov Empire, and in particular the baleful and ultimately disastrous influence of Rasputin at court. The film became controversial by the very nature of its subject-matter, and is remarkable perhaps only in that it presents a far from negative picture of the Tsar, shown here as weak and indecisive, but with positive traits. This film has become something of a landmark, in that it has willy-nilly become part of the Russian search for an idealized and glorious past.

While discussing nationalism in the Russian context, we must inevitably touch on the question of anti-semitism. The anti-semitic brand of nationalism has obviously been prevalent in official circles in Soviet culture throughout the Brezhnev period. Aleksandr Askol'dov's *The Commissar* (1967) was banned for twenty years, ostensibly because of its sympathetic portrayal of a Jewish family looking after a Russian female commissar during the Civil War. Gleb Panfilov's *The Theme* (1979) was banned until 1987, as it featured a long discussion on the Jewish emigration to Israel in the 1970s (a taboo subject in the official media).

The preoccupation with the past, in particular Stalinism, has been a major feature of the culture of the past thirty years or so. The investigation of the crimes and injustices of the past, begun in earnest since *glasnost* but tentatively initiated by Khrushchev in 1956, is an attempt to identify the painful areas of national and collective experience, and is, in films to be discussed below, fundamentally different from the elegiac nationalist preoccupations of Klimov, Shukshin, and others. The attempt to put right the wrongs of the past is a concentration on the facts of history, and not on mirages or myths of some idealized past 'golden age'.

The reappraisal of the more recent past, especially the Stalin years, is to my mind the most important aspect of the search for identity and justice in post–glasnost cinema. For these directors, just like writers and journalists, are interested not in the sufferings of the Russian soul, the idea that to be Russian is to 'feel' Russia and the Russian soul, but rather concentrate on actual facts, events and personalities. The first major film to explore the impact of Stalin's terror on family life was not a Russian film at all. The Georgian, Tengiz Abuladze's *Repentance* (1987), through a mixture of religious symbolism, allegory, and fantasy, offers a relentless picture of the destruction of a family in a police state run by a ruthless dictator, Varlam. But more fundamentally, the dictator's own family are unable to live down the consequences of his tyranny after his death, and Varlam's grandson commits suicide[6]. The relationship of the individual to tyranny has also been explored in *The Servant*, made in 1988 by Mindadze and Abdrashitov. Here the relationship of two men, one an important official, the other his driver, is turned into an allegory of power and submission, for it is not so much the official who imposes his will on his driver (and others); rather the driver has an inner need to be subservient. Is this an explanation for the domination of the Russian people by one man for over a quarter of a century?

Another film that explores the psychological and social effects of Stalinism, but in a recognizably Western format, is Alexander Proshkin's *The Cold Summer of 1953* (1988), where political prisoners do battle with criminals who take over a village, following Beria's amnesty of prisoners in 1953 (shortly after Stalin's death). It is not, however, the (admittedly exciting) shoot-out that is important, but rather the psychological aftermath for the hero. This is Sergei, a former political prisoner, who overcomes his cynicism to realise the value of relationships and human interaction. Indeed, the violence serves as Sergei's catharsis, after which he, like his times, becomes settled and balanced.

Another film that combines the elements of the traditional detective story with historical enquiry is Aleksei German's *My Friend Ivan Lapshin* (1985), a film based on the literary works of Iurii German, the director's father. The plot deals with the local policeman, Lapshin, and his eventual tracking down of a local band of violent criminals, but the film also evokes the atmosphere of provincial Russian life in the 1930s, when the action is set. There is no explicit mention of the historical background, such as collectivization, purges, or mass starvation in the countryside (save for a portrait of Stalin glimpsed towards the end of the film), but the ordinary life of people is portrayed as hard and sometimes brutal. Here people live together in communal apartments, have little or no privacy, and criminals are shot in cold blood by the police. With its candid portrayal of life in 1935, the film undoubtedly has a nostalgic appeal for many Russians, but on a deeper level the director is subverting the socialist realist depiction of reality that his father gives in his stories. Set just before the onset of the Great Terror, the film offers hints of what is to come. Furthermore, the film's plot is narrated retrospectively from the vantage point of the present,

6. Walters, E. (1988), 'The Politics of Repentence: History, Nationalism and Tengiz Abuladze', in *Australian Slavonic and East European Studies*, vol. 2, no. 1 (1988), pp113-142.

thus establishing a broad temporal perspective. Thus, the times live on in the present through memory[7].

A major documentary film in this vein is *Solovki Power* (1988), directed by Marina Gol'dovskaia. Solovki used to be a monastery in the White Sea, founded in the fifteenth century, that became under the Bolsheviks one of the most infamous and brutal camps for political prisoners. Gol'dovskaia's film goes to Solovki, tells of its terrible regime, but, most tellingly, brings into the narrative the first-hand accounts of those who spent time there and survived. Interestingly, it also includes footage of former guards, and shows how they have prospered in the post-Stalin period. It is indeed a harrowing film, and all the more powerful for not overstating its case (or overstaying its welcome).

In the 1970s and 1980s there have been several popular and respected films dealing with life in Russia before the Revolution. What is of interest in these films, is the absence of any explicit ideology condemning the iniquities of that time. Moreover, films based on works by Russian authors, such as *Unfinished Piece for Mechanical Piano*, directed by Nikita Mikhalkov in 1977, *Vassa*, directed by Gleb Panfilov in 1983, and *Cruel Romance*, directed by El'dar Riazanov in 1984, are based, respectively, on literary works by Anton Chekhov, Maksim Gor'kii and Aleksei Tolstoi. Each of the directors displays a reverence for the literary source, both in characterization, and in fidelity to the original plotline, but each film has a contemporary resonance. Mikhalkov's film, in particular, is purportedly about the inner torments and self-doubt of a failed radical at the turn of the century, but it also contains many passages that can be interpreted as an explicit comment on the capitulation of the Soviet intelligentsia in the 1970s. In all of these films it is as if the problems of collective and individual morality, emotional vacuity, and spiritual malaise, prevalent in Tsarist society, were equally true of the modern age. Individual morality is measured against the touchstone of Russian literature of the nineteenth century; these film-makers demonstrate above all a cultural continuity between past and present.

In a different context, an important film is *The Garage*, directed in 1979 by El'dar Riazanov, with a script by himself and Emil Braginskii. It is a satire, a genre very difficult to practice in Brezhnev's Russia, and its target is the selfish materialism of modern Muscovites. The plot revolves around a meeting called in a research institute to decide who is to lose their allocated garage space because of a planned motorway route. In fact, the institute's leadership has already decided on the four people who will lose out, and the meeting is intended merely as a rubber stamp exercise. However, in the course of the evening — and then the night and the following morning, as those present are locked in — not only are the greedy and self-serving instincts of today's intelligentsia laid bare, in varying degrees, but the collective overturns the decisions laid down from on high, and asserts its own priorities. Those who lose out, in the end, are the highly-connected and those in positions of power, and a new order is born. Amid chaos and anarchy (some of it extremely funny), the old elite is overthrown. Thus the film can be seen as an allegory, and a remarkably perceptive and prophetic one, about the revolt of the masses against their leaders, and the removal of the social hierarchy. At the end of the film, the

7. Rifkin, B. (1992), 'The Reinterpretation of History in German's Film *My Friend Ivan Lapshin*: Shifts in Centre and Periphery', in *Slavonic Review*, vol. 51, no. 3 (Autumn 1992), pp.431-447.

last garage space to be lost is decided by drawing lots. In other words, democracy replaces autocracy. It is remarkable that this film was allowed to appear in Brezhnev's time, for it offers a subversive picture of what can be achieved with 'people power'. The world was to be witness to a much greater illustration of this in 1991.

So, too, Russians today grope their way towards an as yet uncertain identity, an unknown destiny. This is an identity not as yet based, as in Western Europe, on political institutions, as these (the Communist Party, the Parliament) have been discredited in the wake of the revolutions of 1991 and 1993. Rather, identity is based above all on culture, and the cultural consciousness is one which 1917 did not break. Russian culture has always been deeply spiritual, and it is perhaps worth pointing out here some films with a clear religious subtext. Larisa Shepit'ko's war film *The Ascent*, made in 1976, offers a picture of a Soviet partisan tortured, and eventually executed, by the Germans, and whose death scene is framed in hallowed light as he assumes a Christ-like aura. *Scarecrow*, directed in 1987 by Rolan Bykov, is the story of the persecution of a girl by her classmates, and her suffering is increasingly seen as a martyrdom[8].

In the years since Gorbachev came to power and effectively ushered in the end of totalitarianism, national identity has been based on the concept of the Russian soul, the cultural heritage, and the belief in the strength and spirit of Russia. For Russians, the collective identity is based on the national experience and the people's culture. Given the cataclysms of twentieth-century Russian history, the assault on its culture by Bolshevik ideology, and the decimation of its people, it is no wonder that the current search for identity and purpose is beset by bitter argument and division. For some, national identity becomes associated with a glorification of the past, the assertion of a mythic, golden age of order, stability, and above all faith in the destiny of Russia. On the other hand, there are film-makers intent on exploring the actual events and experiences of the past in order to put right historical injustices, to avoid a repeat of them in the future. Nobody doubts that Russian cinema now faces an uncertain and difficult future, given the collapse of old institutions and the absence of material support. However, the exorcism of the past, and the search for new meanings and identities, continues apace, as does the inquiry into the cultural identity of Russia. Above all, these strivings offer direction and a sense of purpose for the future[9].

8. Rifkin, B. (1993), 'The Christian Subtext in Bykov's Cucelo', in *Slavonic and East European Journal*, vol. 37, no. 2 (Summer 1993), pp.178-193.

9. For further discussion of cinema in Russia today, see Anna Lawton, *Kinoglast: Soviet Cinema in Our Time*, Cambridge University Press, 1992; Andrew Horton and Michael Brashinsky, *The Zero Hour: Glasnost and Soviet Cinema in Transition*, Princeton University Press, 1992; Julian Graffy, 'Unshelving Stalin: After the Period of Stagnation', in Richard Taylor and Derek Spring (eds.), *Stalinism and Soviet Cinema*, Routledge, London and New York, 1993, Cambridge: Cambridge University Press pp. 212-227.

The critique of reification: a subversive current within the cinema of contemporary Spain

Dominic Keown

For historical reasons which require little elucidation, the coherence and quality of Spanish cinematography were severely prejudiced by the political tribulations which afflicted post-war Europe. The diaspora of the country's creative elite — including the legendary genius of Luis Buñuel — which heralded the advent of Franco's autocratic rule was, in itself, a blow of devastating proportions. The disaster was compounded, however, by the ensuing stringency of a totalitarian regime which strove to suffocate — ultimately through censorship, though primarily through the state-controlled machinery of subvention, investment and licensing — any aesthetic or political statement alien to its ideological and moral persuasion. As a result, when the cinema in other countries, most noticeably in Italy and France, began to recover from the cataclysm of World War II, the cohesion of the experience in Spain was severely impeded[1].

Despite such unfavourable circumstances, however, it would seem reasonable to propose that if Spanish cinema lacks the synchronic coherence of those schools and tendencies which emerged nationally elsewhere on the continent, there is by way of counterbalance, a compensatory convergence at the thematic level — particularly with regard to treatment of the condition of the individual in society — which adds cogency to the experience, belying the initial impression of disparity or fragmentation. Indeed, it is my intention in this essay to illustrate this basic unity of purpose, with special reference to the work of Buñuel, Berlanga and Almodóvar who, despite representing different generations of cineastes, examine this issue in a manner reminiscent of what has become known as the *esperpento*, a creative current endemic to the Hispanic cultural tradition[2].

As might be expected, Luis Buñuel was the first to adapt aspects of this particular creative idiom to the cinema, and there is little doubt as to the additional influence of Marx on the elaboration of his approach. Generally speaking, when assessing Buñuel's ideological affiliation, critics have tended to adduce the vitriolic censure of the bourgeoisie as exclusive evidence of his subversive purpose. Though such an evaluation is not without validity, the ferocity of Buñuel's diatribe against the futile introspection of this class, and its mindless accumulation of wealth, seems to have diverted attention from an equally patent articulation of Marxist theory. I refer, of course, to the area of social philosophy, with particular regard to the corresponding speculation concerning the ontological condition of the individual in the Capitalist system. In this environment, founded on the notion of the contract, humanity is reduced to the status of a commodity in the realisation of a process which assigns a market value to every social

1. Hopewell, J. (1986), *Out of the Past: Spanish Cinema after Franco*, London, BFI, pp.7-43.
2. *Esperpento*, or *grotesquerie*, was the label used by the author Valle-Incl†n (1869-1936), to define his later plays and their deformed representation of character. Its inspiration is the later work of Goya (1742-1828), particularly the Caprichos, where the mimetic depiction of individuals is subject to grotesque distortion, producing a dehumanisation which compromises their integrity and autonomy. It is significant that Berlanga employs the same qualificative to describe his opus.

relationship[3]. Indeed, the effect permeates even individual relationships, with the concept of money being adduced as the ultimate motivator[4]. It is this reduction of the human status that concerns Buñuel from his earliest films onwards.

The topic is initially broached in *L'Age d'or* (1930) in the sequence outlining the pernicious and dehumanising effect of advertising, that bastion of the Capitalist system. On three occasions during his escorted walk through the city of Rome, Gaston Modot is transfixed by images of parts of the human anatomy being exploited to sell goods: hand cream (finger), stockings (legs), and film poster (face). In each case, the image mutates disturbingly from photographic representation to actual human appendage within its configured reality and back again. Buñuel's insistence on the episode, within the visual narrative, clearly underlines the importance of the issue. Human integrity which would be represented graphically by the physical completeness of the body, is violently compromised by fragmentation into isolated units. The force determining this curtailment is the utilitarian impulse central to the capitalist ethic which wantonly exploits humanity for profit and gain. The process of reification implicit in the system, and its violence against the individual, is thus isolated both succinctly and with eloquence by Buñuel's camera.

In fact, corporal disintegration or dismemberment is a favourite motif in Buñuel's evocation of the brutality of the capitalist system, forming a key component in the elaboration of a grotesque idiom. In this case, the contextualisation of the episode within the framework of advertising illustrates concisely the inhibitive effect of the system. Elsewhere, the deliberation is more speculative, alluding to the related compromise of individual autonomy exacted by the strategic institutions of a bourgeois controlled society. In his perceptive gloss on Marx, Althusser indicates how Capitalism ultimately depends not only on the perdurance of the capacity to produce, but also on the continuance of a general 'subjection to the ruling ideology or of the *practice* of that ideology' amongst its members. To this effect, a network of ideological state apparatuses, whose impact is most readily appreciated in the sphere of education and the family, 'crammed every *citizen* with daily doses of nationalism, chauvinism, moralism', and by dint of continuous coercion cajoled individuals into compliance with established precepts[5].

Sensitive to the duress involved in such repression, Buñuel incessantly exposes the reduction in human potential which accompanies the mandatory espousal of the externally imposed norm, repeatedly illustrating the oppressive presence of the models of behaviour insidiously inflicted by bourgeois convention. A pertinent example occurs at the start of the narrative of *Un Chien andalou* (1928) as Simone Mareuil silently contemplates Vermeer's *The Lacemaker*. The juxtaposition of the two offers a visual impression of the interpellative force exacted upon the young woman by this icon of bourgeois adolescence. What is more, the aura of tranquillity which emanates from the lacemaker's placid acceptance of her condition, betrays a submissive conformity which exemplifies the Althusserian notion of subjection; an attitude, it is inferred, which her younger version is being encouraged to embrace.

It is therefore not surprising that the rest of the film should be an

3. Marx, K. (1963), *Selected Writings in Sociology and Social Philosophy*, Harmondsworth: Penguin, p.169.

4. op.cit., Marx, K. 1963, pp.169-170

5. Althusser, L. (1971), 'Ideology and Ideological State Apparatuses', in *Lenin and Philosophy and Other Essays*, London: NLB, pp. 121-173.

entreaty to her modern counterpart to impose her own volition, and reject such behavioural standards. Such an admonition is conveyed as, on a number of occasions, we see Mareuil coerced to comply with the dictates of conventional morality, particularly in the sphere of sexual deportment. First of all, her exaggerated maternalistic response when her companion falls off his bicycle disguises the reality of her libidinal attraction towards him. Likewise, when confronted with his advances, she successfully defends herself with a tennis racket, symbol of bourgeois propriety. When her companion exposes her to the erotogenic realities of mature sexuality, lips, mouth, body hair, and so forth, she reacts with decorous discomfiture, and leaves immediately. However, once these repressive, diversionary modes have been rejected, she can act with autonomy and composure. At the end of the narrative, she is able to enjoy a confident and relaxed physical intimacy with her lover; a far cry from the frantic equivocation previously exhibited in her sexual dealings.

The motif of dismemberment enhances our impression of the restrictions imposed on individuals. *Un Chien andalou* opens with a grotesque act of violence against the human form, which is continued in the recurrent image of a severed hand, trapped in the door, or else poked menacingly by the androgyne. Its relevance is made apparent at the end of the film, as the young man complains that his girlfriend is late. Initially the shot of the watch is truncated at the wrist; subsequently it pans out to reveal the bodies in their completeness. The implication is quite clear: the reduction in autonomy equated with aquiescence to the external norm was reflected in the film by physical diminution. However, when such obeissance is discarded, as when the couple refuse to conform to the dictates of bougeois decency, the body is shown in its entirety. In fact, Buñuel was to employ the same motif to similar effect in *The Exterminating Angel* (1962), where the pastiche of the severed hand sequence from *The Beast with Five Fingers* reflects the guests' unquestioning submission to the etiquette of social norms. Similarly, in *Tristana* (1969), the eponymous heroine's demurring to the repressive strictures of marital orthodoxy is conveyed by the amputation of her leg. The rigorous imposition of externally devised behavioural codes is demonstrated more blatantly in the iconography of *L'Age d'or*. Here the environmental pressure to conform is visually apparent as, in a moment of rare lyricism, Lya Lys — blonde, virginal and pure — is regaled in accordance with the Romantic paradigm of feminine virtue. However, the illegitimacy of the enterprise is exposed, as Buñuel positions her not on a pedestal but on a similarly radiant toilet. The pastiche is completed a few scenes later as, still dreaming of her lover, she nonchalantly dispatches yet another stereotype of the female condition — a large cow asleep on her bed — from her bedroom. As Buñuel's style matures, the treatment of the topic becomes less explicit: the question of an established paradigm acting as a determinant of behaviour lurks below the surface of *Viridiana* (1961), but is foregrounded in the earlier *Nazarín* (1959). Here, a priest (Paco Rabal), implements Christ's teachings and example to the letter and, as the familiar tale is retold, is persecuted, abused, and unjustly imprisoned — just like his predecessor — by a patently hypocritical and capitalistic society.

Curiously, the fate of this virtuous, altruistic figure is presented without the slightest sympathy. Buñuel shows no compassion for his tragic hero, and the inspired denouement concisely conveys the nature of his censure. Nazarín's failing is precisely that he never stops to analyse the reality of a situation before acting. Instead, he conforms uncritically to the Christian model of behaviour. The protagonist emulates the Nazarene (hence the relevance of the name) so completely that he forgoes any individual independence; and Buñuel duly exposes this weakness by his representation of the figure as a pastiche of standard iconographical formulae. The doleful, solemn countenance, the bandaged head suggesting the crown of thorns, the Mexican carabineer reminiscent of Roman soldier, all recall conventional depictions of the agony of Christ, a reference further emphasised by subtle modulations of perspective which immediately recall various Renaissance essays on this subject.

In effect, Nazarín shows himself as little more than a fraud and collaborator. In the final prison scene, his conversation with the Sacrilegist convinces him that the attempted implementation of Christian values — of which his most cherished institution of charity is a fundamental, diversionary component — is an irrelevance. Thus disabused, he marches with determination towards captivity. At this point, however, he is confronted by a crucial dilemma: whether or not to accept the charity (a pineapple) offered him by a sympathetic fruit vendor. His initial refusal represents a determination to reject his previous espousal of values which, as he himself had earlier done, legitimise or perpetuate the injustice of the status quo while changing nothing. Once he accepts the offering, however, he again complies with the strategies of the existing order and, as such, is mercilessly parodied by Buñuel. Nazarín strides out, apparently more convinced than ever about his identity with the king of kings. The masterful final image reiterates the standard icon, which is magnificently subverted as we become aware that the orb of majesty he proudly holds in his left hand is, in fact, a pineapple!

The excessive fervour with which Nazarín endeavours to imitate the standard version of the Christian paradigm whilst being conscious of its vacuity, offers a classic example of Sartrean *mauvaise foi* (bad faith): an affected subservience to the exterior trappings of one's condition, despite recognising the essential illegitimacy of such a posture. In his studied imitation of the Christian icon, Nazarín parallels Sartre's waiter who, in his effusive behaviour, relegates his true being so as to conform to the caricature of his profession as it is demanded by society. Similarly, Buñuel's visual insistence on the exorbitance of Nazarín's mimicry, indicates Nazarín's awareness of the basic fallacy; in Sartrean terms, he must know the truth in order to conceal it[6].

However, by framing this notion within the specific context of a deliberation on the iniquity of Capitalist society, Buñuel adds a Marxist dimension, again clearly revealed in *Belle de Jour* (1967). Here, Séverine (Catherine Deneuve) embodies the reified paradigm of bourgeois femininity. Her husband's revelation that his greatest happiness will be realised when she bears him a child — more precisely, an heir — is a clear example of the chrematistic value imposed on woman in this context, and is entirely consistent with Engels's speculation on the subject[7]. Not only is Séverine a beautiful mannequin to be bought and sold in the brothel, but

6. Sartre, J.-P. (1969), *Being and Nothingness: An Essay on Phenomenological Ontology*, London: Methuen, p.60

7. Engels, F. (1977), *The Origin of the Family, Private Property and the State*, London: Lawrence and Wishart.

she also enjoys the same basic status in her marriage. The same reduction in human worth was expressed previously in *L'Age d'or* by Modot's arrival at the party, menacingly trailing his lover's dress behind him. Similarly, time and again in *Belle de Jour*, we are reminded that the elegance of Sévérine's wardrobe attests to her condition as a commodity[8].

Sévérine's only escape is into the world of sexual fantasy. Significantly, when she realises these activities — which constitute a wholesale rejection of bourgeois morality — and exercises her independence, she takes control of her situation and achieves autonomy. Consequently, the daydreams stop and she assumes the dominant role in the relationship. The standard power structure is thus entirely reversed and, at the end of the film, her crippled husband is reduced to utter dependence on her. Nonetheless, at this moment of individual liberation her infidelity is communicated to her partner and, overcome by guilt, she, like Nazarín, hesitates, and refuses to exercise her new independence, preferring to regress to the escapism of her previous conventional existence.

In a marvellous pastiche of the Hollywood happy ending, one of orthodoxy's most exemplary strategies, Sévérine imagines the complete mental and physical recuperation of her spouse as she enacts — with the exaggeration previously displayed by Nazarín — the role of dutiful wife. According to Marx, it is necessary 'that humanity breaks illusions and tears asunder the "motley ties" that bind man to the old social forms'[9]. However, Sévérine and Nazarín both choose to reject this directive, and instead comply with those Institutions, or 'motley ties', whose repressive and irrelevant nature they had just appreciated. Their alacrity in this regression again recalls Sartrean *mauvaise foi*, with its implicit social critique regarding compliance with behavioural standards.

In this way, in line with two funadamentally Marxist principles, Buñuel establishes the premises for subsequent cinematographic deliberation on the condition of the individual in society. In the first place, a contractual, utilitarian element is revealed as the determinant for every social relationship — even the most intimate. Secondly, this system is shown to compromise any personal fulfilment through the interpellation of its ideological apparatuses whose repressive strategies and paradigms coerce humanity into submission. This curtailment of individual autonomy and consequent dehumanisation is expressed filmatically by grotesque deformation or caricature.

Despite the clear divergence in idiom and vocabulary — particularly at the level of narrative — the same formula could equally be applied to the films of Luis García Berlanga, whose sympathy for, and familiarity with, standard Marxist analysis was made patent in the celebrated Congress of Salamanca in 1955. However, the gentle cynicism, warmth and humanity which characterise his work have often belied the austere resolve of his speculation — frequently more immediate and incisive than Buñuel's — leaving him, inexplicably, with the spurious and misleading label of 'conservative anarchist'[10].

Such an ignominious, contradictory qualification stems, no doubt, from fundamental ignorance of Marx's social philosophy, which is represented with patent orthodoxy in *Plácido* (1961). According to Marx, in the Capitalist system 'only one relationship counts ... that of exploitation', all

8. Therborn, G. (1980), *The Ideology of Power and the Power of Ideology*, London, NLB.

9. Lifshitz, M. (1973), *The Philosophy of Art of Karl Marx*, London: Pluto Press, p.92

10. Hernández Les, J. and Hidalgo, M. (1990), *Conversaciones con Buñuel*, Barcelona: Anagrama.

relationships being governed by self-interest and profit[11]. It would be difficult to imagine a more canonical exposition of this premise than is presented in this film, where every activity is determined by the question of money. Here, the altruistic fallacy of the institution of charity is again caustically exposed as, on Christmas Eve, and during the 'Seat a pauper at your table!' campaign, the eponymous hero (Castro Sendra) rushes headlong in a desperate attempt to pay an instalment due on a *carromotor*, his only means of livelihood. His frantic efforts to settle the bill condition his existence entirely; every action he undertakes is determined by its possible financial remuneration, and every relationship, even the most intimate, involves a detailed calculation of its potential reward.

The utilitarian nature of the charitable campaign is also revealed, as merely a front for an advertising drive promoting the wares of its sponsor Cocinex Pressure Cookers, and the real motivation behind bourgeois patronage is poignantly denounced. There is little altruism; the attraction resides exclusively in the opportunity for ostentatious displays of wealth when bidding for the honour of inviting the poor unfortunates to dinner. The auction itself, in ascribing a monetary value to each individual, is emblematic of the reification of humanity by capital, which is also reflected by Plácido's *carromotor*. Initially, the vehicle transports merchandise, then people, and finally a corpse. Without the slightest regard for dignity, human beings are systematically reduced to the level of cargo. The process is crystallised hilariously by Berlangan in the visit to the bank when finding himself without sufficient funds to effect payment, actually leaves his brother-in-law as collateral security!

The distortion in the representation of character further accentuates the compromise of human integrity. In the opening sequence, Plácido is depicted as a person, but is circumscribed within the format of a cartoon, thus equating his human status with that of a cartoon character. In this important opening he is given bread and wine by some exterior, anonymous hand, not only identifying his condition with that of the paupers in the film, but also emphasising a lack of any real autonomy: he is totally incapable of controlling his own situation.

The diminutive Castro Sendra, and the insistent camera perspective from above, further compromise the stature of the protagonist, a point enhanced by the rudimentary characterisation. As an individual, Plácido is never allowed to develop; the only dimension we see of his personality is the desperation caused by his frantic quest to pay the instalment. As a result, we are given the impression that his existence is determined exclusively by his economic circumstance — a reduction of human integrity which is made further explicit by the inspired choice of title. A certain irony is immediately apparent in the name of the protagonist as, impelled by the contractual obligations of a system he cannot control, he is anything but placid. Berlanga's incisive quibble, however, resides in the fact that 'pagar a plazos' (hence the derivative, Plácido) is the Spanish for hire purchase. As such, a label which should identify a human entity, in reality denotes a condition of subjection imposed by an extraneous system.

The theme of individual disenfranchisement and denial of personal fulfilment is reiterated in the black comedy *El verdugo* (*The Executioner*, 1963) whose protagonist, José Luis (Nino Manfredi), has a single project

11. op.cit., Marx, K. 1963, p.170

for self-realisation: to emigrate to Germany and become a mechanic. However, in an elegant intrigue which exemplifies the interpellation of Althusser's ideological apparatuses, social and family pressures conspire to coerce him into marriage and, since he therefore remains in Spain, into the forced acceptance of his father-in-law's profession of executioner.

Despite his abhorrence of murdering a fellow human-being, José-Luis is relentlessly cajoled by environmental pressures into compliance with his office. Revealingly, the macabre execution scene at the end of the film demonstrates how the real victim of this repressive configuation is, in fact, the protagonist who must be dragged kicking and screaming into the death chamber, and not the criminal, who enters totally unperturbed. Stripped of any autonomy — his attempts to determine his own actions and, ultimately, to resign, being constantly dismissed — José Luis is little more than a commodity: a hangman who must serve his trade. In this he represents all those who labour in the system where the utilitarian ethic converts individual worth into a saleable item, at the mercy of contractual obligations.

So destructively inescapable is such a fate that it is presented as destiny, and is thus hauntingly evocative of Althusser's vision of the 'reproduction of the conditions of production'. A eulogy of hereditary trades at the crux of the film is followed at the climax by the chilling sequence in the water caves in Majorca. The police search for their man in a launch, eerily calling his name through a megaphone. The allusion to the Stygian boatman is patent; but the contemporary Charon comes not for the soul of José Luis, but to transport him to the hellish torment of his fate: the compliant service of his externally imposed profession. The endless coercion of the individual to conform is reiterated in the final scene, as grandfather, father, and son return, in the same boat, to Madrid. The implication of the final image is that the same fate inevitably awaits his child. Thus, the oppression is clearly considered to be pre-ordained.

Not surprisingly, Berlanga's caustic critique denounces not only the utilitarian nature of the Capitalist system but, following the lead of Buñuel, also the interference of behavioural stereotypes. However, his concern is more specifically with the concept of the imposition of a 'national' characteristic. In *Bienvenido Mr Marshall* (*Welcome Mr Marshall*, 1952) and *La vaquilla* (*The Heifer*, 1985), Berlanga highlights the behaviour of his compatriots in what might best be described as a communal demonstration of *mauvaise foi*.

In *Welcome Mr Marshall*, the citizens of a tiny village in Castile are informed that the American delegation, responsible for awarding aid under the Marshall Plan, is due to visit the town. Desperate to impress the visiting dignitaries, and so to benefit from their generosity, the villagers arrange a festive reception. However, rather than greeting their visitors with an authentic display of folk-culture, they decide to attempt the entirely alien Andalusian or *españolista* paradigm of what the foreigner imagines Spain to be. Forsaking their usual attire for that of flamenco dancers, they turn their town into a miniature Seville. With guitars and costume typical of Andalusian *señoritos*, the townsfolk parade about in a fashion as foreign to them as it would be to their American visitors. Like Sartre's waiter, they grotesquely distort the reality of their personality so as to coincide with the accepted stereotype.

Needless to say, the disinterested motorcade speeds through the fairy-tale village without even stopping. Left high and dry, the dejected inhabitants return to their usual routine, but with the added problem of the expense of their extravagant charade. A fundamental change in attitude occurs, however, as the townsfolk reject the world of fantasy to address the reality of their situation, which they analyse and resolve in a lucid fashion, and together they struggle to settle the debt. The Marxist message is clear in Berlanga's call to humanity to face up to the real conditions of life.

It is intriguing to consider *La vaquilla* from a similar perspective. The historical relevance of the film is apparent in its overt appeal for consensus and unity in the wake of the internecine divisions of the Civil War. On a more speculative level, however, the deliberation reverts intriguingly to the theme of compliance with stereotype, which was a feature of *Bienvenido Mr Marshall*. At the beginning of this war film — in which not a shot is fired — the soldiers in the front lines are bored. Two years into the conflict the two sides no longer fight but tolerate each other with some humour, communicating via a loud speaker system. Their mutual dependence is suggested by the frequent exchange of articles, such as tobacco, and cigarette papers, which are not available on the other side. As a consequence, the overall impression in this bellic situation is, paradoxically, one of convergence and productive cohabitation.

The tranquillity is destroyed, however, by the arrival of the heifer, and the announcement by the Nationalists of a projected fiesta complete with bullfight. In a fit of pique, the Republicans make a bungled attempt to steal the beast, as a result of which it is killed in the minefield. As a historical allegory, the implications are clear. The animal, an archetypal symbol of Spain, is destroyed by two polarised factions whose intentions are to expropriate and possess it exclusively. As such, the narrative constitutes a straightforward admonition to Spaniards to reject factionalism and participate collectively in the management of their patrimony: the alternative is mutual destruction.

On the other hand, the symbolic value of the animal is somewhat ambivalent; the beast comes to represent not only Spain, but also its customary male characteristics of virility, intransigence, and violence. Its presence actually provokes the Republican soldiers to abandon their peaceful existence and to behave in a fashion consistent with the conventional and externally imposed code of machismo. The original attitude of circumspection, mutual self-preservation and collaboration — a sensible reaction to the perils shared by all on the front lines — are superseded, in the shadow of the bull, by an excessively masculine pattern of behaviour. Individuality is sacrificed in a collective indulgence in rank *españolismo*: the caricature of the national, male personality.

Berlanga is keen to emphasise the antagonistic tendencies at the level of character. On the one hand we witness the stereotypical *braggadoccio*: virility, jealousy and bullying typical of machismo. On the other, in a more intimate and personal vein, the soldiers also relish the opportunity to emphasise their individuality, as evinced by their gleeful performance of their previous occupations. It is not insignificant in this respect that each setback suffered by the Republicans coincides with an episode of *machista* behaviour: the affray caused by the suspicious boyfriend, the *imbroglio* occasioned by the visit to the brothel, the problems resulting from the hollow boasting of the erstwhile *matador* and so forth. In contrast, the expression of their own particularity is rewarded by the successful resolution of the problems which their compliance with stereotype had caused.

Their misguided escapade ends in catastrophe, leaving the party stranded precariously in 'no man's land'. As might have been anticipated, their deliverance coincides with the destruction of the bull in the minefield; it is only at this point that they abandon their macho antics and return safely to camp. In the end, this mindless display of bravado is duly castigated by the commanding officer who, indulging in his obsession with depilation, shaves the soldiers heads. The biblical allusion is clear. The fracas of the macho-inspired raid is punished by removal of hair, conventional emblem of virility and masculine strength, those characteristics which, in Berlanga's opinion, had caused the hostility.

In addition to functioning as historical allegory, the film offers an equally intriguing speculative dimension. Just as in *Bienvenido Mr Marshall*, the protagonists are distracted from facing the reality of their situation, and are sidetracked into following a diversionary and externally imposed code of conduct. In both cases Berlanga exposes the catastrophic results[12].

At first reading it may appear somewhat incongruous to consider the work of Pedro Almodóvar within the framework of Marxist-inspired meditation on the condition of the individual in society. Champion of the licentiousness of the *Movida* of the 1980s, including the discarding of intransigent, catholic morality — particularly in the sexual sphere — combined with *pasotismo*, the spontaneous rejection of the pious, self-righteous sobriety of the anti-Franco struggle, his films seem passionately unconcerned with such ponderous speculation. Indeed, his films could be described with some legitimacy as flippant essays in self-referentiality: the crystallisation of the jocular spirit of postmodernism.

However, there is not the slightest doubt that Almodóvar owes much to his native predecessors in terms of formulation and presentation of theme. Despite its extravagant idiom, *¿Qué he hecho yo para merecer esto?* (*What Have I Done To Deserve This?*, 1984) deals with the miserable existence of an impoverished proletarian housewife, Gloria (Carmen Mauraand) and her desperate struggle to make ends meet to provide for her two children, with precious little help from her taxi-driving husband. However, once again — and consistent with Buñuel and Berlanga — the intention might have been lifted verbatim from the *Communist Manifesto*: bourgeois morality has reduced the family relationship to a purely financial level. Nothing could be clearer in an ethos where money acts as determinant for every activity. Even in the home, the members purchase food and drink from the grandmother. Indeed, the extremity of the situation is shown with a true Buñuelian flourish as Gloria, faced with financial ruin, nonchalantly sells her son to a paedophile dentist!

The presence of the prostitute Cristal (Veronica Forqué) reflects the stratagem employed in *Belle de Jour* to emphasise the utilitarian or monetary

12. It is important to remember that, in contemporary Spanish history, Machista precepts are exclusively associated with the Right and its leaders (Primo de Rivera, José Antonio, Franco, Tejero etc.). Compliance with a standard of 'national' male deportment therefore has clear political ramifications, whose dangers this film reveals.

basis of family and social relationships, particularly in the case of women. Just as Séverine/Belle is exploited equally by husband and clients, Almodóvar removes the smokescreen of moral respectability to reveal that any putative superiority of housewife over hooker is, in fact, an illusion. The similarity of their condition is repeatedly exposed, epitomised by Gloria's remunerated participation with Cristal in Chávarri's rendition of machista exhibitionism. Indeed, her son's activity as a rent boy further underlines their common fate and, as in *El verdugo*, intimates the perpetuity of the situation.

The ensuing reduction in human integrity is conveyed by the standard formula evidenced thus far. Although Almodóvar employs the favoured Buñuelian technique of dismemberment, to express the limitation of individual autonomy in *Matador*, he favours here the possibilities offered by perspective, photocomposition and symbolism. Gloria is repeatedly depicted as imprisoned in the home; her lack of independence is emphasised by a series of shots taken from within washing machines and other household items, which circumscribe and constrain her actions. Her lack of freedom is clear from the opening sequence as she is entrapped in a split-screen shot, and appears as an appendage, grotesquely excentric in her parody of the male-centred activity of the kendo school which is shown centre screen.

A similar truncation of personal autonomy is evident in *Atame* (*Tie me up! Tie me down!*, 1989), but in this case Almodóvar digresses from the overt chrematistically inspired violence against the individual, so patent in *¿Qué he hecho?*, to speculate on the familiar and related theme of the compromise of human liberty by the imposition of stereotype. As porn star and odd job man respectively, Marina (Victoria Abril) and Rikki (Antonio Banderas) are streetwise, shrewd, and self-sufficient. Marina's integrity triumphs over the machista threat posed by her ageing film director, and the advances of Oscar the Space Beast who would drag her off by the hair to his cosmic cave. Similarly, Rikki rejects the advances of those in authority who seek to control him — epitomised by the director of the asylum — and survives the rigours of the modern underworld through astuteness and ingenuity.

The free-living couple, however, regress into orthodoxy as Rikki falls for Marina and, following convention, insists that she become the mother of his children. The bonds with which he binds her to the bed, reminiscent of the same motif in *Viridiana*, are merely the exterior representation of those ideological apparatuses which cajoled José Luis in *El verdugo* into rejecting his personal ambition and complying with the status quo. Marina, instead of analysing her situation, submits to the paradigm offered, inviting Rikki to subject her further. Although the ties that bind her at the end of the film are invisible — her need to act as dutiful spouse — she drives off to find her partner in what will, significantly, constitute another happy ending, we are reminded of the extravagant dissimulation of the protagonist at the climax of *Belle de Jour*. The song the two intone on the way back to their conventional relationship, *Resistiré* (I will resist), poignantly throws into relief their sacrifice of autonomy, and their compliance with the repressive values of social orthodoxy.

Significantly, the outcome is anticipated graphically through a series of motifs pointing to conformity with the paradigm. Throughout the film, as in *Nazarín*, there is an insistence on religious icons, particularly the images of Jesus and Mary, whose ideological content, representing the conventional ideal of the nuclear 'Holy Family', reflects the interpellative drift of the narrative. Moreover, red and blue — the colours traditionally associated with these figures — recur insistently on the screen. This impingement of iconography on reality is anticipated in the opening sequence, as the painting of the asylum actually dissolves into the building it represents, recalling the same imposition of artificial norms upon the reality of the individual.

This externally formulated compromise of integrity is, in turn, accentuated through symbolism. The collection of models and puppets which inhabit the bedroom where Marina is entrapped is poignantly analogous to the reduction in autonomy which she will concede. Like the figurines, Marina does not function of her own volition but is manipulated by an exterior force. A similar impression is evoked in the grotesque choreography of the musical sequence where grandmother, mother, and daughter mindlessly dance to the same tune like marionettes, again suggesting that the repressive coercion of the protagonist and her sex will be inevitably reproduced from generation to generation.

The topic is handled with greater sophistication, however, in *Matador* (1986), where the bullfighter and paragon of machismo, Diego Montes (Nacho Martínez), turns lady-killer on his retirement from the ring. Despite the seductive allure of his protagonist, Almodóvar (like his predecessors) underlines the curtailment of independence which this abject compliance with stereotype presupposes. The wooden monotony of Nacho Martínez's performance recalls the unidimensional austerity of Cassen's characterisation of Plácido. Similarly, and with clear echoes of Buñuel, the willing compromise of human integrity is evoked by physical disability, in the lameness of the bullfighter and the detective. In this respect, the chain-saw amputations which excite the protagonist onanistically in the opening sequence, graphically evoke the reduction in integrity presupposed by the espousal of the code of violence against women, the determinant of his behaviour throughout the movie. The coincidence in style and purpose with the presentation of the theme of stereotype in *Un Chien andalou* requires little comment.

Montes's partner in sado-masochistic delight, María Cardenal (Assumpta Serna), becomes his equal in every aspect. A seductress of the proportions of a Hollywood vamp, her murder rate of unsuspecting males rivals that of the *torero*. Various critics have argued with some coherence that Cardenal's power over men exemplifies the superior condition of women in post-Franco Spain, following the sexual equality act of 1981[13]. Whilst there can be no doubt of the pertinence of such an interpretation, the implications of this representation take relevance beyond the limitations of specific historical context.

Rather than exercise her independence freely, as was the case of Marina in the early part of *Atame*, María blindly imitates a stereotypical pattern of behaviour which complies exactly with the representation of female destroyer, *femme fatale* or siren: the paradigm of woman as imagined by decadent Romanticism. The iconographical influence is forcefully

13. Evans, P. (1993), 'Almodóvar's Matador: Genre, Subjectivity and Desire', in *Bulletin of Hispanic Studies*, LXX no. 3, July 1993, pp.325-335.

emphasised by the director as he consciously adorns and attires his protagonist so as to recall the sphynx, chimera and female exterminators inhabiting the decadent world of French Symbolism, in particular the work of Puvis de Chavannes and Gustave Moreau[14].

The compromise entailed by such uncritical adherence to standard precepts is further enhanced by the theme of predestination. The star-crossed lovers enact their suicidal ritual against the backdrop of an eclipse. Moreover, the repeated sight of two concentric circles, a dominant motif in the film, recalls the markings on hallowed ground prepared for magic rites, accentuating the function of procurement associated with their celebration. The sense of inevitability is also underlined by the sharp perspective, created by insistent downward shots, which constrain the characters and make their actions seem externally controlled. It is almost as if the director, like his predecessors, is warning us that subscription to externally imposed modes of conduct will inescapably lead to the total destruction of personal freedom and integrity.

In this way, the work of the three directors examined in this essay indicates a solidity of purpose and style at the heart of the cinematographic experience in Spain. Each director exposes the utilitarian value placed on personal worth in capitalist society, and denounces the constraint this imposes on the integrity and possible self-fulfilment of individuals. In addition, each examines the strategies by which the bourgeois state, particularly in the area of the imposition of standards of behaviour, seeks to cajole its citizens into compliance with these norms. Recourse to iconographical reference, whether by pastiche, essay, or straightforward stereotype, is repeatedly adduced to underline that imposition upon human autonomy is an inescapable component of the system.

What is more, the aesthetic representation of this phenomenon further unites the trio. Their characters, impelled by environmental pressures they are unable to control, actually appear as sub-human playthings in the grip of an exterior force. Their one-dimensional personalities reveal only the exasperation inflicted by their actual circumstances, so they are constantly on the verge of a nervous breakdown. This deficiency is enhanced by the use of perspectives which compromise their completeness, and frequently reduces them to mere figures of fun. In fact, we often look down on them — for instance in the opening sequences of *Plácido* and *¿Qué he hecho?* — as we would the animated figures in a cartoon.

Though many of their contemporaries, especially Bardem and Saura, are concerned with the same theme, the creative idiom they adopt is qualitatively different. In their exposition, it is usual for characters to be represented as well-rounded individuals, enjoying the same mimetic status as the audience and, as such, the ensuing response is neither humorous nor dispassionate but rather, affective involvement. Betsy Blair's magnificent performance in *Calle mayor* (*Main Street*, 1958), as the ageing spinster trapped in the misogynistic claustrophobia of small-town Spain, brings the audience to tears. Similarly, the raw violence of the protagonists in *La caza* (*The Hunt*, 1965) provokes the spectator's indignation.

The creative voices of Buñuel, Berlanga, Almodóvar are, however, more latent in inspiration. Their objective is not to elicit emotive empathy or antipathy for their protagonists, but to open our eyes to our own condition.

14. Keown, D. (1992), 'Ethics and Aesthetics in Almodóvar's Matador', in *Hispanic Studies in Honour of Geoffrey Ribbans*, Liverpool: Liverpool University Press, pp. 345-353.

In a consciously cerebral manner, which recalls Brechtian *Verfremdung*, their films encourage us to perceive the distortion of human potential effected by Capitalism. As such, their creative stance is essentially subversive, not only in its critique of the repressive nature of the system but also in its uncompromising aesthetic refusal to allow us the comfort of a conventional affective relation with their characters[15]. Berlanga's celebrated war-cry illustrates, with characteristic disdain for propriety, the committed, critical, and seditious stance shared by all three:

15. Buñuel, L. (1982), *My Last Breath*, London: Fontana.
16. Cited by Diego Galán in *Diez palabras sobre Berlanga*, Teruel, Instituto de Estudios Turolenses (1990), p. 14.

When I said that this society is shit, I don't know if I insinuated any alternative or wholesale solution or even if I offered any constructive thought. I've said elsewhere that me and my cinema are sailing in the same boat as this society. What I'm trying to do on board, is to keep on peeing in the same place, so that maybe I can open up a hole which will end up by sinking the boat[16].

Current problems in the study of European cinema and the role of questions on cultural identity

Ian Aitkin

According to Anthony Smith, transformations in collective identity result from traumatic developments which 'disturb the basic patterning of the cultural elements which make up the sense of continuity, shared memories, and notions of collective identity'[1].

Therefore, the issue of collective identity generally arises during periods in which existing patterns of cultural cohesion begin to fragment, and disparities appear between established cultural stereotypes and emerging social, political, and economic circumstances. These emerging circumstances are what Smith calls 'traumatic events', and it is these which must be defined, in order to develop an appropriate explanatory framework for understanding the ways in which transformations in the representation of collective identity appear within cultural production. One imperative, therefore, in attempting to understand a body of cultural production, such as European cinema, in relation to questions of identity, is the development of a theoretical framework within which the representation of collective identities can be assessed, both with regard to European cinema in general, and to the study of particular films. One useful theoretical model is that of 'globalisation'.

Globalisation, the development of a global economic, political, and ideological culture, is frequently cited as a primary cause of contemporary crises within established conceptions of national identity. It has been argued that the increasing inclusion of nations within capitalist economic and political relations, and liberal ideological paradigms, has been responsible for the three most important events in recent European history: the revolutions of 1989, the fall of Communism, and the implementation of the single European market. These events, it is argued, can be seen as both significantly determined by, and providing a radical acceleration to the process of globalisation.

According to the theory of globalisation, an intense burst of economic, political, and ideological global integration occurred after the Second World War, under the hegemony of the then dominant world power, the United States. Commentators, such as Gilpin[2], have seen this as facilitating the international growth of democratic systems, and as initiating the beginnings of a benevolent global society. In the same vein, and writing shortly after the partial collapse of communism, Fukuyama has talked in terms of the 'end of history', and the triumph of liberal values[3]. Similar sentiments have also been expressed in relation to the hegemonic role of Hollywood within international cinema, where, it is argued, the intrinsically liberal and democratic values embodied within the Hollywood film

1. Drummond, P., Paterson, R. and J. Willis, (eds.) (1993), *National Identity and European Cinema*, London: BFI.
2. Gilpin, R. (1987), *The Political Economy of International Relations*, Princeton: Princeton University Press.
3. Fukuyama, F. 'The End of History', in *The National Interest*, no. 16, pp. 3–18.

challenge the totalitarian control of the media by various national, authoritarian, and state regimes. Such views of the merit of Hollywood's hegemony are often linked to populist notions that American films transcend the self-interested objectives of national political establishments, and speak directly to the people, giving them what they really want.

However, other writers, such as Wallerstein (1984) have viewed the process of globalisation more pessimistically, in terms of Marxist and post-Marxist theories of cultural imperialism, where culture is seen as the ideological instrument of economic and political exploitation. Schiller has also pointed to the hegemonic, superstructural function of American media interests after the War[4], and the Macbride Commission has argued that the growth of American interests in the third world and Europe has led to the subjugation of regional, ethnic, and minority cultures[5]. These criticisms of American hegemony have also led to the emergence within European and international cinema, of various counter-culture cinema movements, one of whose primary functions has been to challenge the domination of Hollywood films.

It is generally accepted by most commentators that following the relative decline of American hegemony caused by the rise of Japanese and European economic power, another phase of extensive global, cultural integration took place from the 1970s onwards. This occurred within the context of the development of new communications technology, political deregulation, and the growth of new media conglomerates. In Hollywood, the major studios were absorbed into huge international conglomerates such as Gulf and Western, Coca-Cola, Sony, News Corporation, Turner Broadcasting Systems and Matsushita. A new form of international integration emerged within the cinema industry, in which audio-visual hardware companies such as Sony and JVC linked up with software producers and distributors such as Columbia-Tristar, MGM and others. This meant that films could be produced and distributed for a greatly increased international market, using the new distribution media of cable and satellite.

The rapidly accelerating transnational environment is most evident at the economic and political level, with transnational institutions such as the World Bank, the GATT, the G7, the IMF, the EU and NAFTA increasingly regulating international affairs. However, it is also apparent at the ideological level, with the emergence of ideologies which express the new economic and political priorities and stress the desirability of a consumerist individualism.

The occurrence of these international processes of integration was accompanied by the disintegration of national configurations, in response to the twin pressures of economic internationalisation, and internal sectarian conflicts. As Giddens has remarked, transnational integration, national disintegration, the rise of marginal movements, and the re-emergence of nationalism around new ethnic and political configurations, are all associated with the accelerating process of globalisation[6]. In Western Europe the process of globalisation within national states has been limited by the existence of nationally organised structures, forming barriers against both the increased flow of international capital into the national cultural space, and the demands for autonomy from minorities within. By

4. Schiller, H. (1969), *Mass Communication and American Empire*, Kelley.

5. MacBride Commission (1980), *Many Voices, One World*, Unesco/Cogan-Page.

6. Giddens, A. (1990), *The Consequences of Modernity*, Cambridge: Polity Press.

reinforcing national systems of power, and conceptions of national identity, structures such as publicly funded cinema and broadcasting not only restricted globalisation, but also helped to sustain national public service cultures, founded on relatively stable concepts of collective national identity. In this sense, public service culture sustains an essentially nineteenth-century conception of national identity, in which an effective 'imagined community' could be addressed in terms of images of the sovereign nation state. Culture is thus defined in specifically national terms, as embodying the 'vernacular repertoires of myth, memory, symbol and value' associated with the common culture[7]. In Europe, France has been at the forefront of attempts to defend national culture against the inroads of globalisation. The recent French-inspired victory at the Uruguay round of the GATT, represented an important, though surely temporary, defence against globalisation. This meant that subsidies to European cinema were allowed to continue, on the grounds that films and audio-visual material have a special national-cultural status.

As the pace of globalisation increased from the 1970s onwards, and institutions founded on conceptions of national culture were further eroded, the basis of classical nationalism, the congruence of national culture and polity was increasingly undermined[8]. As the social structures of Western Europe became gradually more integrated into an international market-based system, the logic of capitalist production and consumption affected previously protected cultural media, such as public service broadcasting, and nationally subsidised cinema. Deregulation of the media in countries such as Italy, has led to major changes in the way that national identity is represented; for example witness the emergence of Berlusconi and Forza Italia.

A number of consequences have resulted from this shift, including an increase in the array of market forces and in the imperatives of consumerism, operating within the general field of national cultures within Europe. Theodore Adorno and Max Horkheimer's initial conceptualisation of the 'culture industry' as a system which effectively reproduced the interests of a ruling capitalist class, may have been overly pessimistic in relation to the critical potential of popular culture. However, their premise can still be drawn on today to explain how the growing influence of internationally-driven market forces and consumerism has led to a breakdown of social democratic structures, to the relative impotence of a critical avant-garde, and to the increased commodification of culture[9].

The growing intrusion of an international logic of consumerism and commodification into the European public sphere has also resulted in a deconstruction of the central mythic figure of nationalism: the unitary collective subject. As Gelner and Kedourie have argued, the characteristic feature of eighteenth-century notions of identity, was that of the unitary subject, able to understand the world through the realisation of his/her own innate capacities of reason[10]. Theories of national identity effectively superimpose onto the nation state this rational and libertarian conception of the unitary subject, which realises its innate essence and personality through processes of communication, introspection and social interaction.

The unitary subject of the Enlightenment has long been called into question. This has been done firstly by various forms of nineteenth-century

7. Smith, A. (1990), 'Towards a Global Culture', in Featherstone M. (ed.), *Global Culture*, London: Sage.
8. Gelner, E. (1983), *Nations and Nationalism*, Oxford: Blackwell.
9. Adorno, T. and Horkheimer M. (1972), *The Dialectic of Enlightenment*, Herder and Herder.
10. op.cit., Gelner, 1983

determinism (Darwinism, Marxism, Positivism and theories of genetic and environmental determinism), secondly by various forms of twentieth-century relativism (including post-structuralist, philosophical relativist and post-modernist theories). All of these emphasise the volatility, rather than unity, of the subject. Clearly such an attack on the conception of a unified subject has important implications for traditional theories of national collective identity and, in certain cases, for national cultures. On occasion it has been used as part of a political strategy to attack existing nationalisms, whilst, ironically, retaining the myth of the collective subject to advocate the establishment of new emerging conceptions of nationalism, and new nations. Within the domain of cinematic representation, this division may lead to the emergence of assertive national cinemas, which emphasise the notion of a national collective subject, in parts of Europe which have recently carved out new identities: in the Baltic states, Ukraine and in the former Yugoslavia. This division has also led to a relative withdrawal from representations of the national, or even the macro-political, in the less confident and more intellectually fractured cinemas of Western Europe.

A crucial influence on European cinema today therefore, is this commercialisation of the European public sphere; the model of globalisation provides a framework for examining that influence in terms of the new conceptions of collective identity which it suggests. European films can be studied in relation both to the issues raised by globalisation, and to how those issues are articulated within either a given national cinema, or the films of particular film-makers. A number of provisional thematic motifs which are related to globalisation and to changing configurations of national identity can, therefore, be provisionally identified within European films. These include motifs such as the expression of anxieties about national identities (*The Nasty Girl*, 1990; *Remains of the Day*, 1993); the affirmation of particular national identities (*Chariots of Fire*, 1981; *Henry V*, 1989; *A Room with a View*, 1986; and possibly *Heimat*, 1985); or the expression of anxieties about supra-national identities (*Europa*, 1990; or *Prague*, 1991); while films such as *1492* (1992) affirm such identities, exploring the new transnational and pan-European market configurations. A whole series of films, including *Chocolat*, 1989; *Time of the Gypsies*, 1989; *The Crying Game*, 1992; *Naked*, 1994; and *Riff-raff*, 1992, deal with the segmentation of national and supra-national identity, in terms of cultural minority, stateless nation, class, gender, ethnicity or the colonial. The construction of a 'national identity' for a largely home audience, underlies films such as *Jean de Florette*, 1987; while the construction of a national or European identity for a foreign, and predominantly American audience, is revealed in films such as *Swann in Love*, 1985, and *The Big Blue*, 1988. In other films, narrative cohesion, linear plot, and reference to a concrete social reality are replaced by a more generic, stylised rhetoric illustrated by recent French films including *Diva*, 1982, and *Subway*, 1985. Other motifs include the representation of an ambivalent relationship between the individual and the local, national or supra-national sphere; the legitimation of established collective identity through the use of history, a sort of 'retro' mode of cultural tourism, illustrated by films such as *Tous les matins du monde*, 1993, or *Le Château de ma mère*, 1991, or the ironic use of the past to cast doubt on the foundational myths of the nation, such as *A*

Handful of Dust, 1988; *Babette's Feast*, 1987, *A Month in the Country*, 1987; *Fanny and Alexander*, 1983; *Jean de Florette*, 1987. Finally, we can cite the revival and resuscitation of existing genres as the linking of trans-European marginal identities, or of marginal identities within nations; the decline of critical, hard-hitting film-making; the creation of new genres, built on comic and melodramatic elements, targeted at the European market and the synthesis of national broadcasting genres into a transnational product.

This complex of thematic motifs and characteristics can be examined across particular films and groups of films, and referred back to the underlying concept of globalisation. The value of this approach is that it affords a set of theoretical categories which can be broadly applied to national and European cinema. The disadvantages which might stem from an injudicious use of the model, result from its possible schematic and superficial application. Such an application, however, can be avoided. How, for example, does *Jean de Florette* use the past to justify national identity, how does it interrogate that identity, how does it represent marginality, how does it compress space and time, what is the function of naturalism, how is historical irony and the representation of the individual, the local and the national expressed, what — to use Corcoran's terminology[11] — are the 'selectors' used to figure French identity? These are complex questions which require careful study of the film itself, but the model of globalisation, and the assumptions about representations of identity which it implies, does at least allow these questions to be framed in a relatively systematic way.

I want now, to turn briefly from the general to the particular, and to apply some of these issues to an analysis of representations of collective identity in Kenneth Branagh's film version of *Henry V*.

Henry V, Shakespeare's most patriotic play, was first produced as a film in 1945, when Britain was engaged in a world war. The question arises as to why Branagh should produce such a play, steeped in national crisis and triumphalism in Britain in 1989. The empirical explanations available are that Branagh had played Henry V for the RSC in 1984, and that when he left the RSC to found the Renaissance Theatre Company, with the aim of popularising Shakespeare, he believed that *Henry V* would make a popular and successful film, given its combination of romance and action[12]. However, these elements of personal biography and directorial intention do not adequately explain why *Henry V* was made in the way it was. In order to understand this better, we must address the ideological discourses conveyed in the film, and relate them to a context.

Henry V is one of the most difficult of Shakespeare's plays to adapt into a contemporary film. This is because its overt nationalist and royalist ideology will be read as something approaching propaganda by a modern audience. The play becomes accessible, and most germane, at moments of national crisis such as the Second World War, when the only previously filmed version was made. Yet Branagh's *Henry V* was made at a relatively untroubled period in the late 1980s, during the later stages of Thatcherism, and before the outbreak of the revolutions of 1989. Some simplistic explanations may be provided, such as the project developed over a period of time, until it was ready for production in 1988. However, it could also

11. Corcoran, F. (1993), 'Nationalism, Identity and Social Memory', *Media Development*, vol. XL. no. 4.
12. Branagh, K. (1989), *Henry V Screen Adaptation*, London: Chatto and Windus.

be argued that the film's thematic content closely resembles the dominant ideological discourses of the late Thatcher period.

These discourses, emphasising entrepreneurialism, libertarianism, chauvinism, xenophobia, and a boorish nationalist individualism, are best illustrated in the characterisation of Henry, Essex, Bardolf, Nimm and Pistol. Here, however, the first of many confusions within the film is revealed, for no distinctions are made in terms of these values, between Establishment figures such as Henry, and members of the criminal underclass, such as Bardolf. In the film, the discourse of nationalist individualism transcends discourses on responsible citizenry and legality, just as entrepreneurialism superseded questions of social responsibility within Thatcherism. The film defines responsible citizenry in terms of individualism and nationalism, rather than of a moral code of values relating to social interaction. Similarly, the question of legality is subordinated to questions of individual and national necessity. One of the points I wish to argue here, is that the 1988 version of *Henry V* articulates an essentially confused and contradictory ideological discourse, combining an array of Elizabethan, Victorian and Thatcherite values, which are enmeshed within a humanist and realist reading of the play.

Another important contradiction within the film occurs between a discourse of rampant nationalism, and a discourse of transnational accommodation. The film effectively ends with a brokered negotiation between Henry and the French King, mediated by the Duke of Burgundy — perhaps the medieval equivalent of Jacques Delors? A new, transnational European order emerges out of this negotiation, and these images of pan-Europeanism coexist unsettlingly with the nationalist rhetoric in the rest of the film.

However, this confusion between nationalism and pan-Europeanism — which may reflect the widespread British ambivalence towards the European issue at the time — is amplified by the means by which the new order is established, not by amicable agreement, but by invasion and military victory. The resolution is enforced by British might, not by a pan-European set of protocols. There is a strange similarity here between Henry's bluff and uncompromising dealings with French leaders, and Thatcher's railings against Delors and the Commission during the 1980s. Indeed, the film's final scenes resemble contemporary conservative aspirations for a European future, under confident British ideological directorship. In this sense, the film seems to offer a form of reassurance about Britain's relationship to the European Union, based on the certain victory of British strength and character over European bureaucracy. In other words, the film offers a fantasy which both reaffirms traditional notions of how Britain should deal with the 'problem' of Europe, and seeks to disguise the real relationship between a peripheral Britain and a powerful European centre in the 1980s. The film offers a reassuring vision of a strong England, and distorts the reality of the growth of central European powers (the Franco-German alliance) during the 1980s. In terms of its representation of collective identity therefore, the national character is presented as both victorious, and as setting the terms of the European agenda.

The film returns to one of the sources of English national identity —

its military strength and glorious past. It does this not in order to search for the origins of present ideological inadequacies, as a film such as Bergman's *Fanny and Alexander*[13] does, but in order to draw strength from that source, in an admittedly complex and contradictory, but ultimately uncritical way. No critique of origins is mobilised here, and the fundamental nationalist myths of race, spirit and folk are strongly reaffirmed. The film uses realism to affirm mythic aspects of the English character by naturalising ideology. Realism combines with the myths of archaic Englishness, and modern (Thatcherite) ideologies of Englishness, in order to make those myths accessible to the nation in the 1980s; a nation which is used to relating conventions of realism with notions of truth. The film reaffirms the virtues of common sense, ordinariness, hard work, hostility to intellectualism, sophistication, and foreigners, loyalty to one's leaders and belief in the intimate relationship between one's individual identity and the national identity. This is the roll-call of British national stereotypes which was mobilised so effectively by Thatcherism during the 1980s.

This use of ideology and realism distinguishes the film fundamentally from Olivier's 1945 version, which attempted, wherever possible, to subtly parody the nationalist ideology of the play. It is surely significant that, in 1945, during the struggle with Nazi Germany, Olivier chose to parody nationalism, whereas in 1988, when there was no national crisis, Branagh chose to give that ideology a contemporary articulation through the use of realist conventions. Realism thus performs a dual function: naturalising the nationalist ideology, and providing it with a humanist dimension. The interconnected themes of humanism, realism, and nationalism, however, often fail to work together. For instance, in the set speeches where Henry addresses his army, where it is unclear whether we are witnessing humanist declaration (discourses about 'human' requirements of action and struggle), nationalist rhetoric (discourses about the necessity for national triumph), or psychological realism (discourses about the problems of an individual caught within the force of events). Elsewhere in the film, the force of the nationalist rhetoric overwhelms any attempted realism.

The film also uses a strategy which forms an increasingly common aspect of the marketing of European films today, and is implied by the globalisation model, which places an emphasis on packaging the cultural heritage as a commodity with inherent cultural capital. To this end, *Henry V* uses representations of royalty, pageantry and feudalism; the legacy of Shakespeare, symbol of Europe's cultural and literary excellence; reference to great European events (Agincourt) and the exploitation of historical locations. *Henry V* was designed in order to popularise Shakespeare. It was co-produced by the BBC as part of its strategy of defining an export niche for itself, based on its role of expressing British culture and heritage; whilst popularisation is not necessarily problematic, it must be recognised that if bereft of critical substance, it can be associated with processes of commodification and globalisation.

Henry V does include some representations of marginal characters, but these are never systematically differentiated from the dominant national or feudal order in a way which would suggest a substantially fractured society. A basically unitary conception of the nation is emphasised, even though at the time of Agincourt in 1415, there were persistent peasant

13. Bergman's exploration of history is intimately connected with a sense that the problems of the past still affect contemporary Swedish culture

revolts against forms of feudal exploitation. In the play itself, questions concerning the legitimacy of feudalism are posed, even if indirectly. *Henry V* followed a trilogy of plays, *Richard II* and *Henry IV* Parts one and two, which explored the legal and moral legitimacy of feudalism and absolute monarchy. However, rather than continue this debate, the 1989 film focuses on internecine struggles within the establishment, redirecting attention away from deeper structural divisions. Branagh's attempt at political realism stops at a neo-pluralist conception of social and political debate. The debate is one in which politics is defined in terms of a struggle between elites, which allows the film to dwell on issues of individual characterisation, rather than on social and political issues. This may be seen as both a failure of the film's professed realism, and a product of the nationalist ideology which underscores his version of *Henry V*.

In conclusion, it is evident that this initial synopsis of the film requires more detailed analysis. The argument that *Henry V* mobilises a confused synthesis of the nationalist discourse developed by Thatcherism in the 1980s and images of a pan-European new order, that the relationship between these two is premised on the domination of the latter, and that realism functions both to naturalise nationalism and to endow it with a humanist dimension — needs to be qualified by further textual analysis and contextual information, concerning factors such as co-production strategies, authorial intention, and historical influences. Nevertheless, there are grounds for regarding the film as a profoundly conservative text, which challenges the dynamic of globalisation through a strident re-assertion of British national identity.

Any use of globalisation as a model for the study of European cinema must, as we have seen, involve historical and sociological contextualisation, and the empirical study of aspects of production, distribution, exhibition and finance. Moreover, it requires an awareness of both individual and collective agencies within the processes of film making. All this goes beyond the specific question of identity, and locates that question firmly within a context of more contextual studies. What is at issue, is the best use of abstract theoretical models, in conjunction with intermediate and empirical modes of enquiry, into European film texts and contexts. That is the challenge for those attempting such macro studies of European cinema today. What the model of globalisation provides is a series of categories relating to questions of the representation of individual and collective identity in films, and this series of categories can provide a framework in which to examine the content of films in greater detail.

Film and Northern Ireland: beyond 'the troubles'?

Brian Neve

Only time will tell whether the republican and loyalist cease-fires of 1994 will continue to hold, and whether the 'peace process' will gain real momentum. The 1990s saw an increase in film representations of 'the troubles', and this article surveys this work, and assesses its significance. To what extent do the cinema and television dramas of this period transcend the much criticised portrayal of the conflict by the news media? Do they reproduce or challenge the dominant myths and symbols which contribute to the way that the conflict is imagined and constructed, by insiders and outsiders alike?[1]

Critics of British media coverage of Northern Ireland have pointed both to journalistic routines that decontextualise violence, presenting it as cause rather than effect, and to constraints on the news media, imposed by successive British governments[2]. A study of *New York Times* reporting of the 1980s criticises coverage that emphasised 'a sectarian conflict between recalcitrant religious groups', while its author remembers editorial disapproval of her efforts to investigate 'questionable shootings' by police and army undercover units — the so-called 'shoot to kill' policy[3]. David Miller suggests that the professional imperatives of news journalism tend to make violence the main 'rationale for reporting Northern Ireland'. However, he points out that the content of the British media is not simply dictated by official sources, and that a liberal section of the British press, in particular current affairs television journalists, played a leading role in the campaign to expose as unsafe the convictions and imprisonment of those thought responsible for the Guildford and Birmingham bombings[4].

Much of the literature dealing with filmic representations of the Ireland question has also stressed the cliched iconography of the conflict, and the tendency to see violence and 'terrorism' as cause rather than effect. John Hill, in his analysis of British and American films dealing with Ireland and with 'the troubles', argues that such work consistently ignores or underplays the political and social context of the conflict. Carol Reed's *Odd Man Out* (1947) is seen as casting a long shadow, given the recurrence of passive protagonists overwhelmed by insuperable forces. In *Cal* (1984), for example, the central figure, echoing the western outlaw who cannot re-enter society, is a victim who is destined to pay a personal price for his marginal involvement in a sectarian killing. Paramilitary violence is seen as criminal rather than political, private lives are centre stage, and there is no resolution other than the order imposed by the RUC and, implicitly, by the British state[5].

From a republican perspective, Ronan Bennett is generally unimpressed with recent film representations of the question, finding that such drama still reproduces a clichéd picture of the conflict in the North of Ireland:

'an irrational and bloody slaughter without solution', involving

1. Street, J. (1994), 'Political Culture — from Civic Culture to Mass Culture', *British Journal of Political Science*, 24, pp. 95-114.
2. Curtis, L. (1984), *Ireland: The Propaganda War: The British Media and the Battle for Hearts and Minds*, London: Pluto Press.
3. Thomas, J. (1991), 'Toeing the Line: Why the American Press Fails', in Rolston, B. (ed.), *The Media and Northern Ireland: Covering the Troubles*, London: Macmillan.
4. Miller, D. (1993), 'Official sources and "primary definition": the case of Northern Ireland', *Media, Culture and Society*, 15, pp. 395, 400-401.
5. Rockett, K., L. Gibbons & J. Hill (1988), *Cinema and Ireland*, London: Routledge, pp.150, 177, 181-184.

psychopathic paramilitaries, innocents caught up and unable to break free, and the army and RUC holding the ring[6].

Brian McIlroy refers to a 'fatalistic aesthetic' as characteristic of the predominant genre treatments of the issue in the Thatcher era, but also writes of absent or stereotypical representations of the Protestant community[7]. For independent community film-makers 'No Surrender' and 'Ulster Says No' are not easy to dramatise, and emphasis has tended to be placed on Catholic rather than Protestant women. Bill Rolston has noted the different messages of Belfast and Derry murals, and the more positive and forward looking Catholic iconography[8].

Eamonn McCann, who has himself taken a highly committed view of the conflict, has argued that a liberal model of news and current affairs television that stresses balance and seeing both sides is inadequate as a source of information on the conflict. To tell the story like that, he argues, 'you're trying to tell it from somewhere exactly midway between the two communities ... you're telling it from a place where nobody lives'[9]. Yet it is by no means certain that political filmmaking requires such a perspective. *Battle of Algiers* (1965) may have reflected its makers' sympathies, but its political insight came from a rigorous analysis of the forces on both sides and their rationales.

New contacts between the British government and Sinn Fein since 1990 have arguably weakened the dominant 'anti-terrorist' paradigm, even before the dramatic events of 1993-4[10]. In addition, the complex structures of society and culture in the North of Ireland have been increasingly documented in the work of writers such as John Whyte (1991), Desmond Bell (1990), Steve Bruce (1994), Fionnuala O'Connor (1993), and in the Cultural Traditions Group and the Opsahl Report (Pollak, 1993). The Broadcasting Ban of 1988, together with the media's increasingly confident challenging of the convictions of the Guildford Four and the Birmingham Six, encouraged the use of the drama documentary technique in such productions as RTE's *Dear Sarah*, Granada's *Who Bombed Birmingham?*, the BBC's *A Safe House*, and Yorkshire Television's *Shoot to Kill* — all of which were broadcast in 1990. While the dividing line is not always clear, such drama documentaries are generally better discussed in relation to current affairs journalism, and are therefore excluded from this survey.

Several medium or larger budget films of the 1990s have broken away from the traditional perspectives. Far from blaming the Irish, *Hidden Agenda* (1990), directed by Ken Loach from a Jim Allen script, places the blame on the British state. Universal's *In the Name of the Father* (1993) offers no analysis of the conflict as such, but its critique of British institutional racism against the Irish in a particular case is all the more powerful for being carried by a high budget Hollywood mainstream work. In contrast, *Patriot Games* (Paramount, 1992), uses the Northern Ireland conflict as a post-cold war backdrop, pitching 'international terrorism' against Jack Ryan and the American family.

Hidden Agenda and *In the Name of the Father* both raise fundamental questions about the relationship between Britain and Ireland. Twice in the 1970s Ken Loach and writer Jim Allen had been involved in aborted projects on Northern Ireland: the BBC cancelled a play on the politics of the Official and Provisional IRA, and a proposed film on Britain's 'last

6. Bennett, R. (1994), 'An Irish answer', *The Guardian – Weekend* supplement (16 July 1994), pp. 6-10 & 55.

7. McIlroy, B. (1993), 'The Repression of Communities: Visual Representations of Northern Ireland during the Thatcher Years', in Friedman, L. (ed.), *British Cinema and Thatcherism*, London: UCL Press.

8. Rolston, B. (1987), 'Politics, painting and popular culture: the political wall murals of Northern Ireland', *Media, Culture and Society*, 9, pp. 5-28.

9. McCann, E. (1993), 'Telling the Troubles', *The Late Show*, BBC2, TX 21 September.

10. Miller, D. & G. McLaughlin (1994), 'Reporting the Peace in Ireland'. Paper presented to *Turbulent Europe*. Miller, D. (1994), *Don't mention the War: Northern Ireland, Propaganda and the Media*, London: Pluto Press.

colonial war' failed to raise sufficient finance[11]. *Hidden Agenda* was also difficult to finance, and the British production company, having failed to attract television support, turned to America[12]. The resulting film is a conspiracy thriller, which recalls the post-Watergate dramas in the United States, and even *JFK*, in its attempt to create a counter myth for recent British history. The often absent relationship between the British state and Unionist dominance in Northern Ireland is central here, but with the British security state looming so large as an issue, the Northern Ireland debate is left unbalanced[13].

Loach's film is conventionally constructed, unlike the more complex *JFK*; the narrative flows from an early 1980s 'shoot to kill' murder, by British security forces, of an American civil rights lawyer, and traces this to the concern of the British security services to cover up their efforts to destabilise the Wilson and Heath governments in the 1970s. In contrast to a more typical Loach and Allen collaboration such as *Raining Stones* (1993), the grand political design seems too often to dominate the characters; a number of mini-lectures, on Chile, Orange Parade 'tribal rites', Kissinger and the CIA, and the eight-hundred-year-old fight for independence, call attention to themselves.

The difficulty of the form of the conspiracy thriller is that it requires both an incorruptible investigator, and if the conspiracy is to be convincing, a sense that his or her efforts are futile. The plot at times betrays these contradictions. For example, is the fearless Inspector Kerrigan really likely to be so easily daunted by the less than totally convincing blackmail evidence, and would Harris, the MI5 agent turned whistle blower, really hand over the all-important tape on O'Connell bridge in Dublin, rather than send it to the press? While Loach is suggesting that the RUC is manipulated by the British establishment, his film benefits from Jim Norton's performance as the senior RUC officer Brodie. Brodie's passion in dealing with the investigator from across the water, cuts across Allen's rather 'closed' script and suggests something of a Unionist interest which is distinct from that of the British state. But generally, in terms of the light shed on Northern Ireland, one critic argues that the film 'has nothing more to say than that in attempting to defeat terrorism, the special forces have recourse to methods as reprehensible as those of their adversaries'[14].

Jim Sheridan's credits before *In the Name of the Father* (1993) indicate his interest in Irish themes and Irish identity; as well as directing *My Left Foot* (1989) and *The Field* (1990), he wrote the script for *Into the West*. On the subject of *In the Name of the Father*, Sheridan has said that the American backers were interested in the father-son relationship, but less in the 'injustice story' until Daniel Day-Lewis signed up for the project[15]. The resulting film concentrates on the essentials of Gerald Conlon's real experience as a member of the Guildford Four, but its departure from the factual record led to criticism by those who would have preferred something nearer to British television drama documentary style[16]. The simplification is most damaging in the court room scenes and in the picture of the British police, judicial and political authorities, where too much dramatic weight falls on one senior detective (whose name, Dixon, ironically recalls the benign constable in the long-running BBC series *Dixon of Dock Green*).

11. op.cit., Curtis, L., 1984, pp.153-154
12. Geniès, B. (1990), 'Kenneth Loach on the Irish Turmoil', *Le Nouvel Observateur* (10-16 May, 1990), p. 77.
13. White, J. (1993), 'Hidden Agenda and JFK, Conspiracy Thrillers' *Jump Cut*, 38 (June 1993), pp.14-18.
14. Glaessner, V. (1991), 'Hidden Agenda', *Monthly Film Bulletin*, 684, 58 (January 1991), p. 19.
15. Sheridan, J. (1993), interview in *Film Ireland*, 38 (December 1993), p. 12.
16. Kee, R. (1989), *Trial and Error*, Harmondsworth: Penguin. Kee, R. (1994), 'In the Name of the Father', *The Sunday Times* (6 February 1994), Section 9, pp. 3-4.

Audiences can invest the film with their own politics, but the focus stays throughout on Conlon's personal redemption and triumph over British oppression, and on his relationship with his father. In the voice-over, part of Conlon's testimony to his solicitor, he describes himself as a 'paddy thief'; the early scenes in Belfast, where he is threatened with knee-capping by the IRA, establish him and his father as the most unlikely of paramilitaries. Pete Postlethwaite, the harsh father in *Distant Voices, Still Lives* (Terence Davies, 1988), here suggests first the weakness and then the strength of Guiseppi Conlon, while Daniel Day-Lewis supplies a star performance which undoubtedly strengthens the personal focus of the drama. The overall effect is political, in the sense that Sheridan's film countered whispering campaigns from official circles that were designed to cast doubt on the overturning of the Guildford Four convictions in 1989[17].

The prison scenes depart little from received genre conventions, but the episode involving the IRA man's assault on a warder is crucial in separating the film's attack on British prejudice from any endorsement of the IRA. Conlon crucially rejects McAndrew as a false father, returning to a recognition of his real father's strengths. Terry George, Sheridan's Belfast-born collaborator on the script, has said that 'McAndrew is an allegory for where the IRA campaign has taken them'[18]. In terms of the representation of McAndrew as a terrorist, there is no political rationale for the flame-thrower attack. Don Baker, in the role of McAndrew, appears politically dedicated rather than psychopathic, and although the film unconsciously refers to the Irish republican tradition of prison victimisation and martyrdom, it does not endorse it[19]. Martin McLoone reads the prison scenes as more crucial to what he sees as a submerged political analysis in the film. He argues that the rejection of McAndrew is 'a rejection of his chilling and uncompromising politics'[20]. Some Irish audiences may recognise that these prison scenes were filmed at Kilmainham Jail, Dublin, where the leaders of the 1916 Rising were executed. Audiences are prompted to identify with Conlon's triumph in populist terms, as an Irish success story, but an apparently intended analogy between father and son and Britain and Ireland is only weakly supported in the film. The one scene that speaks to the colonial relationship is that in which Gerry Conlon says goodbye to his father as he sets sail for England. Set at night, the steam and lights on the ferry help to suggest a rite of passage that is universal, mythical rather than particular — a story of sons leaving Ireland. As Guiseppi Conlon tells his son to 'Go and live', it is perhaps here that Sheridan gets nearest to suggesting a lack of self confidence — a legacy of colonialism — at the heart of Irish identity.

Following the pioneering and vital work of Channel Four in the 1980s the BBC has increased its commitment to feature film drama in the nineties[21]. Further, producer choice and the BBC's strengthened commitment to regional drama have increased the role of BBC Northern Ireland Drama. RTE has been criticised for not playing a role similar to that of the BBC and Channel Four in the financing of feature film production[22]. However, the BBC — and particularly BBC Northern Ireland — faces political pressures which may affect the type of film that is made. For a 'national region' of the BBC there is a possible contradiction between

17. Bennett, R. (1993), *Double jeopardy: The Retrial of the Guildford Four*, Harmondsworth, Penguin.
18. Cunningham, F. (1994), 'Taking the name in vain', *Fortnight* (February 1994), p. 42.
19. O'Toole, F. (1993), 'A theatre of war', *The Guardian* (18 December 1993), p. 26.
20. McLoone, M. (1994), 'In the Name of the Father', *Cineaste*, 20, 4 (October 1994), pp. 44-47.
21. Cooper, R. (1994), interview in *Film Ireland* (August/September 1994), pp. 20-22. Saynor, J. (1992), 'Writer's Television', *Sight and Sound*, 2, (7 November 1992), pp. 28-31.
22. Rockett, K. (1994), 'Culture, Industry and the Irish Cinema', in Hill, J., McLoone, M., & Hainsworth, P. (eds.), *Border Crossings: Film in Ireland, Britain and Europe*, Belfast: Institute of Irish Studies/BFI and Film Ireland (June/July 1994), pp. 18-21)

regional and broader public service obligations. Should BBC Northern Ireland try to construct or encourage a national, British consensus in a community where nationality is highly problematic, or reflect these divergent national traditions[23]. Budgetary constraints may limit the range and type of film drama, while more commercial productions and co-productions, some with theatrical releases, may also result in more stereotypical depictions of particular cultures. Furthermore, the regional perspective, perhaps influenced by the perceived success of Channel Four, has led to an emphasis on the writer's contribution.

You Me and Marley (BBC North, 1992), explores the youth culture of contemporary West Belfast, examining the relationships between the young, their parents, community leaders and the IRA. The script is by the playwright Graham Reid, who ten years before had authored the 'Billy' 'Plays for Today'. Despite Reid's authority, and the consultation with teenagers in West Belfast, the 'plague on all your houses' perspective creates a negative, despairing portrait. In this sense it makes an interesting comparison with Margo Harkin's view of Derry in *Hush a Bye Baby* and with Joe Comerford's *High Boot Benny*.

There is little sense of a political cause which still has roots in its community. Far from becoming paramilitaries, the youngsters depicted seem largely alienated from an adult world that is brutal, irrational and without authority. The priests are cynical, and at a community meeting one of them tells Reggie Devine, a local boss and ex-IRA Chief of Staff, that the delinquent kids are 'your monsters'. Devine himself seems to doubt the old certainties, arguing despairingly that the local joyriders are 'sons of comrades', and that some of them are 'orphans of men who died for Ireland'. A mother tells him: 'I remember the old days when we were all in this together, whenever the Brits used to raid us'. At the end of *A Matter of Choice for Billy* (1983) the Protestant protagonist left for England to marry a Catholic girl; here the strongest of the Catholic boys leaves for England, while his girlfriend, together with the other Catholic working class women, stay on to cope and pick up the pieces.

Force of Duty (Pat O'Connor, BBC, 1992) presents a character study of a flawed, middle-aged RUC detective at the end of his tether, following the sectarian murder of his long time colleague. He is a Protestant who remembers cheering Ireland on at Landsdown Road against England ('We lost that day too'). He is presented in no man's land, a target for the republican paramilitaries and equally reviled by traditional Unionists, and some in the RUC who would support their own paramilitaries. An officer who has provided information to the loyalist paramilitaries is discovered and thrown out of the force; he is seen more as a 'rotten apple' than as representative of a broader institutional opinion. This represents a liberal British consensus view, and a notion of the nobility and loneliness of authority, but does not exhaust notions of the political significance of the RUC.

The BBC's Screen Two season of 1993-4 included four films which were either set in the North, or were concerned in part with 'the troubles'. *All Things Bright and Beautiful* is set in Cookstown, Co Tyrone in the 1950s — although it was shot in the South — and deals with the problems of a ten year old[24]. The film trades on a carefully reconstructed past, and tells a

23. McLoone, M. (1993), 'A Little Local Difficulty? Public Service Broadcasting, Regional Identity and Northern Ireland', in Harvey, S. & K. Robins (eds.) (1993), *The Regions, the Nations and the BBC*, London: BFI.

24. Written and directed by Barry Devlin, the film was primarily financed by BBC Northern Ireland, with Irish Film Board participation.

comic story of small town pretensions and fears. The Catholic Church
looms large, especially in the young boy's imagination, and politics, in the
form of a passing IRA man and the hated 'B-Men', is at the margins of
the action. This is a film that is set in the North but which plays on the
archetypes of Irish drama, of rural life and the Church. But for the middle-
class Catholic boy the key influences are seen to be those of the radio
culture, from children's songs like 'Nellie the Elephant' and 'The Ugly
Duckling' to the dawning of Radio Luxemburg. Unlike the nightmares
of *Hush-A-Bye-Baby*, those of the BBC film are placed safely in the past,
part of the passing phase of childhood. The combination of Irish symbolism,
and the songs so vividly remembered by English baby boomers is unusual;
it suggests that for some middle-class Catholics, as well as Protestants,
Northern Ireland may indeed have had much in common with Finchley.
The long term political implications of Unionist hegemony remain largely
off camera.

Henri (1993), from a script by John Forte, is also a realist study of
childhood socialisation, but in this case it concerns a Protestant growing
up in contemporary Belfast. The story depicts a young middle-class
Protestant girl from the country who, as a talented piano accordion player,
wins a weekend at a youth music festival in Belfast and is billeted with a
working class family. The tension arises when Henri (Henrietta) innocently
offers, on her unfashionable instrument, Orange Marching songs as
competition pieces.

What is challenged is a mixture of the defensive, bed-rock culture of
loyalist marching songs, and the dour middle-class sensibility associated
with pompous letters to provincial newspapers. The female-headed,
working-class Catholic family that Henri discovers in the city is altogether
more relaxed and self-confident. The association of the bellicose myths of
the marching songs, summoning up the well-worn images, with a young
girl stepping tentatively across class and sectarian boundaries, is quietly
subversive[25]. Henri cautiously learns some new tunes, but sees playing
them in public as a breach of loyalty to her father, master of an Orange
lodge. The film goes no further than this, and the fanciful ending points to
the difficulty of Henri's dilemma.

The BBC/US co-production *The Railway Station Man*[26] begins in Derry,
with Julie Christie as Helen Cuffe being widowed when, as she later
explains to her son, a 'red hot freedom fighter shot the wrong man'. The
bulk of the film is thereafter set in the isolated splendour of Donegal,
where Helen both escapes the past and — to the annoyance of her son,
Jack — discovers a more fulfilling life. Helen's cautiously developed affair
with Vietnam veteran Roger Hawthorne (Donald Sutherland) is centre
stage, reuniting the two stars of *Don't Look Now*, but the climax indicates
not so much that there is no escape from politics but that Helen must
continue to seek such escape by cutting herself off even further from
society. The American is compared to the ageing, ailing Marshal at the
end of *High Noon*; he has made his stand, and wants no more to do with
community.

There is some recognition of a wider politics in the discussion between
Helen and her son. When she talks of a 'violent and illegal organisation',
Jack refers to 'words used by newspapers', and accuses her of 'bourgeois

25. Bell, D. (1990), *Acts of
Union: Youth Culture and
Sectarianism in Northern
Ireland*, London:
Macmillan.

26. 1993, directed by Michael
Whyte, and with a
screenplay by Shelagh
Delaney from the novel by
Jennifer Johnston.

complacency'. Yet the film provides only two forms of commitment, one involving personal obsession — restoring railway stations, painting, falling in love — and the other, involvement with the Provos, which leads only to meaningless violence and death. Politics descends on Helen and Roger's rural idyll in the form of an IRA figure who is totally focused on the wider struggle — a false father for Jack in terms of the narrative of *In the Name of the Father*. The paramilitary survives, but the closing explosion leaves Helen Cuffe alone; she is isolated as the camera flies away from her house by the sea. Unlike the nationalist film tradition, the feminist thrust of the book and the BBC film is clearly separated from the politics of Ireland.

The BBC's *Love Lies Bleeding* (1993) provides a more central and detailed examination of paramilitary culture in the North, while depicting it as part of a wider society. Even here there are motifs that are familiar to films dealing with Northern Ireland. Conn Ellis (Mark Rylance) is a hunger striker serving a twelve-year sentence for murder who has detached himself from direct involvement in the republican struggle. His obsession is with a murdered girl friend — an age of innocence recalled by home movie memories — and the film charts his journey of revenge on one day's 'home leave', in search of the assumed loyalist paramilitary killers. But the protagonist, suggesting the world of *film noir*, is both seeker and victim; he is never in control of events, and the audience shares his increasing disorientation.

From the opening credits, with the loud, 'bleeding' orange of the title, followed by the understated 'by Ronan Bennett' designation, the mix of genre and documentary realism is uneasy. The weakness of the main female role — Conn's partner cum minder, played by Elizabeth Bourgine — may be a result of the BBC's production association with Telecip Paris. The climactic blood bath also undermines the sense of political outcome — as the political struggle between two factions of the Provisional IRA over talks with the British government is resolved militarily — although the effect is unusually to show violence as a consequence of politics. The strength of the film is its depiction of a believable social and political context for the violence. The mobile cameras follow the protagonist into well-barricaded clubs and pubs on each side the sectarian divide, constructing a plausible world of politically committed Belfast. The depiction of a Republican club on the Falls Road — a rabbit warren of alarms, security doors, and secret meetings — helps to demystify the movement and illustrate the implicit and explicit support for the 'armed struggle'.

The origins of 'the troubles', from the arrival of British troops in 1969 to internment in 1971 and Bloody Sunday and Direct Rule in 1972, have come under little dramatic scrutiny. BBC Northern Ireland's *A Breed of Heroes* [27] is set in the Belfast of 1971 and presents a view of the broadening conflict of the time through the rituals and experiences of a number of British army officers, in a battalion of airborne Assault Commandos. A consequence of this perspective is that little context is provided as to the reasons for the conflict, and few Irish voices are heard. To one critic every Irish person depicted falls into one of three categories: 'wild-eyed rioter, hysterical abuse shouter or tart (potential or real)' (Collins, 1994) [28].

27. Directed by David Lawrence, and scripted by Charles Wood from an Alan Judd novel.
28. Collins, M. (1994), 'A Breed of Heroes', *Film Ireland*, 43 (October/November 1994), p. 34.

What the film has to say is mainly about the British army in general, rather than about the nature of the emerging conflict as a whole. Yet only the eccentric Colonel seems sufficiently interesting in terms of a familiar army character drama, while as a visceral 'war film' it ultimately lacks scale, and a sense of the issues involved. Its status as black comedy, and thus its claim to make a more considered judgement on the war than that of the British army at the time, rests rather uncertainly on the film's title and on the performances of Nicholas Farrell as the CO and Richard Griffiths as the drunken tabloid hack.

The tradition of politics and art based around the Nationalist community and dealing with feminism and republicanism has been a strong one, as have the specific problems encountered by Catholic women. These are represented in such films as *Anne Devlin* (1984), as well as various documentaries and shorts. The Derry Film and Video Workshop was created in 1984 as a direct response to what was seen as the superficial and sensational nature of media representation of the North of Ireland, and Ireland in general. Channel Four support was crucial to the production of *Hush-A-Bye-Baby* (Margo Harkin, 1989), the last Workshop production and one which provides a positive, unapologetic view of a group of working class Derry girls, and of the Bogside community in general. The intention of such underfunded work is to represent communities often ignored by the dominant media; to Harkin her film was 'not meant for consumption in Britain'[29]. Despite this, the tone of the film suggests something of the irreverence of *Letter To Brezhnev* (1985), but what is distinctive is the ever-present, if never overstated, sense of an obstructed Irish identity in the North.

The 'troubles' are off-camera, although they provide the constant background to everyday life as we follow a fifteen-year-old Goretti, as she develops a friendship with Ciaran at a Gaelic class. When Ciaran is later taken to Castlereagh to await trial, this takes place suddenly and off-camera; it is something that Goretti has to come to terms with. As with other representations of the North, women are seen as stronger as they deal with the 'big issues' of life, while men — if not fighting — are often seen passively watching television. In providing a picture of everyday life, the film also satirises British efforts to address what they see as the big picture. When the young couple are stopped by a British soldier, the subtitles reveal that Ciaran talks to him in meaningless Gaelic; however, to Ciaran's surprise the soldier replies in the Irish language, and goes on to ask him 'What impact the troubles have had on Irish social, political and economic life?'. The hard edge to the film is provided by Goretti's fears and religious nightmares about her pregnancy. Religion has meaning, and is oppressive. Goretti and her friend Dinky make their observance to a shrine to the Virgin Mary during their trip to Donegal, but on the way back Dinky looks at the effigy and shouts 'Don't you fucking move.' As Martin McLoone points out, the irony is that the services available to Goretti in Derry are 'immeasurably better' than those she would enjoy in Donegal[30].

Channel Four, with its rather different public service brief, has also invested in a number of films which emphasise questions of minority culture and identity. *December Bride* (1990), is Thaddeus O'Sullivan's version of the Sam Hanna Bell novel of the early fifties. The film presents the turn

29. McLoone, M. (ed.) (1991), *Culture, Identity and Broadcasting in Ireland: Local Issues, Global Perspectives*, Belfast: Cultural Traditions Group, Institute of Irish Studies.

30. McLoone, M. (1990), 'Lear's Fool and Goya's Dilemma', *Circa*, 50 (March/April 1990), p. 58.

of the century Ulster Presbyterians as settlers, close to the land, in a way that subverts the general associations of the land with Catholic Ireland. The starkness of life in turn of the century Strangford Lough, in the North of Ireland, is captured by the French cinematographer Bruno de Keyzer, and O'Sullivan has talked of how he had in mind Northern European film-makers such as Bergman and Dreyer, and 'the feel that they had for the land and its people'[31]. In the drama of a young woman's life there is both a sense of the restrictive power of environment and culture, and the possibility of individual autonomy. Fintan O'Toole[32], saw the film as a 'remarkable political achievement' which restored 'a richness and complexity to a history that has been deliberately narrowed'.

The Irish director Joe Comerford has also dealt with the Northern Ireland question in the films, *Reefer and the Model* (1988) and *High Boot Benny* (1993). Martin McLoone has seen the first of these films as 'a new imagining of the national in which the marginal is dominant'[33]. A 'family' of outcasts and outsiders is brought together on a battered trawler, and although they are often self-destructive the motley crew is sometimes successfully presented in lyrical terms. One of the characters is an ex-IRA paramilitary, and the story, which concludes with the consequences of a raid on a bank, can in part be seen as a play on American genre treatments of political outlaws, or outlaws who are political. Comerford tries to connect the political and the personal. He does this through the unconventional love affair between Reefer, leader of the group, and the female Model, leads to a bizarre, pessimistic conclusion in which the Model, the strongest character in the piece, aborts her baby.

High Boot Benny also plays on the use of a loose, un-nuclear family as a metaphor for the unhappy and unproductive situation in the island of Ireland. The film was received controversially in Ireland, with David Butler calling it a 'no punches pulled, pro-republican statement' and a 'narrowly sectarian vision of culture, identity and outlook'[34]. The conflict of the contemporary North is viewed in the circumstances of an austere, seemingly mythological place that is in fact the border country of Donegal. Joe Comerford has commented that the film 'is really about the struggle to remain a neutral entity in a war zone'[35].

Certainly the film's setting is sufficiently bizarre as to weaken the logic of the piece, which is designed to show how young men like Benny become followers of the IRA. All other cultural influences on Benny's identity are removed in the controlled, bleak *mise en scene* of an isolated and neglected border school. By creating a barren world, Comerford abstracts in one sense from the everyday realism of urban accounts. Instead Comerford's use of landscape and elemental forces suggests the allegorical, and hardly sectarian significance of the drama: the failure of dissenting traditions to present a viable and sustainable alternative to the gun.

Without fundamentally challenging John Hill's analysis, many of these more recent films construct a more complex view of the North, and emphasise questions of identity and culture. Neil Jordan's *The Crying Game* (Palace/Channel Four, 1993) is perhaps a special case, but it can be argued that it rounds up but rearranges the usual suspects, as its thriller form is transformed into something nearer to an auteurist puzzle about all forms of loyalty and identity. In the fable of the scorpion and the frog, told first

31. O'Sullivan, T. (1991), interview in *Time Out* (2 February 1991), p. 27.
32. As quoted on the cover of the most recent edition of *December Bride*, Blackstaff Press, 1991.
33. op.cit., McLoone, M., 1990, p.50
34. Butler, D. (1993/94), 'High Boot Benny', *Film Ireland* (December 1993/January 1994), pp. 30-32.
35. Comerford, J. (1993) 'Imagining Ireland', brochure for conference (29-31 October 1993).

by Jody and then by Fergus, his IRA jailor, the scorpion reverts self-destructively to its 'nature', despite its assurances to the frog. In that sense Fergus, while sympathetically played by Stephen Rea, is a familiar figure in film representations of the troubles, the terrorist who finds that he no longer has the heart for killing. It is Fergus's IRA colleague Jude, who conforms to the old stereotype of the female terrorist who is completely dedicated and without feeling. Fergus develops an affection for Jody, the black British soldier he is responsible for keeping hostage, and this leads him to 'escape' to London. The reasons why he joined the IRA are not explained in any depth, although he tells his prisoner that 'you guys shouldn't be here'. Thereafter Fergus does not so much escape from politics into private life as find a different kind of politics[36]. In one sense Fergus is redeemed by his acceptance of a prison sentence on behalf of Dil, but in another his loyalty prompts — if one accepts the conceit — a questioning of all our imagined communities and the identities on which they are based.

36. Zizek, S. (1993), 'From Courtly Love to The Crying Game', *New Left Review*, 202 (November/December 1993), p. 107.

Peripheral visions: film-making in Scotland
Duncan Petrie

The identification, let alone the evaluation, of something that might lay claim to the description 'Scottish cinema', presents the critic with a peculiar quandary. How do we begin to talk about a culturally and economically peripheral sector of what is itself a marginal entity? Ever since the major withdrawal of American finance at the beginning of the 1970s, British cinema has been proclaimed dead so frequently that it has come to resemble something of a zombie: occasionally reanimated by the commercial or critical success (more often than not in America) of one or two films, only to sink back into its more usual catatonic state when the hype dies down[1]. If a viable, to say nothing of vibrant, indigenous film industry cannot be sustained in the UK as a whole, what chance does Scotland (to say nothing of Wales or Northern Ireland) have?[2] The evidence seems unequivocal when we consider that over the last five years only seven feature films, with any claim to being Scottish, have been released: *Venus Peter* (Iain Sellar, 1989); *Play me Something* (Timothy Neat, 1989); *Silent Scream* (David Hayman, 1989); *The Big Man* (David Leland, 1990); *Prague* (Iain Sellar, 1992); *Soft Top Hard Shoulder* (Stefan Schwartz, 1993); *Blue Black Permanent* (Margaret Tait, 1993). Moreover, all of these depended to varying degrees on funding from British (i.e. London based) organisations such as Channel 4 and the BFI.

Film remains an extremely expensive commodity requiring considerable levels of investment, which are correspondingly difficult to sustain in a small country such as Scotland with a limited domestic market, itself a sub-set of another limited domestic market. In addition, the increasing global dominance of the Hollywood product in the latter half of the twentieth century, particularly in Europe, has rendered the possibility of viable alternative 'national' cinemas more and more remote. The much lauded European 'art' cinemas of the post war period: Italian Neo-Realism, the French Nouvelle Vague, the New German Cinema of the 1970s, were all dependent to some extent on the support of governments determined to preserve a space for national cultural expression through cinema in the face of increasing Americanisation of mass popular culture.

This struggle has largely been lost, despite the tenacity of the French Government in the recent GATT talks, and the idea of self-contained national cinemas in Europe has been replaced by a plethora of co-production strategies and pan-European schemes, such as the MEDIA programme supporting 'European' cinema. This in itself raises various questions concerning cultural identity and representation which I am unable to explore in this essay but which have been examined in detail elsewhere[3]. Meanwhile, American films continue to dominate exhibition circuits throughout Europe. If sustained production has become problematic in the major centres of European cinema — France, Italy and Germany — then this is exacerbated in the continent's smaller peripheral nations such as the low countries, Scandinavia and Portugal.

1. For example nothing less than a 'renaissance' in British cinema was heralded after the Oscar triumphs of *Chariots of Fire* and *Gandhi* in 1982 and 1983 respectively. A few years later, the industry was back in the doldrums. A similar (if less hyperbolic) 'buzz' has greeted recent success stories such as *Howard's End*, and *Four Weddings and a Funeral*.

2. It is worth noting that features made in the Republic of Ireland such as *My Left Foot* (Jim Sheridan, 1989), and *The Snapper* (Stephen Frears, 1993), are also often included in British figures. While in economic terms Ireland is closely tied to the British film industry, this is obviously more problematic with regard to questions of control over the means of cultural expression and representation.

3. Petrie, D. (ed.) (1992), *Screening Europe: Image and Identity in Contemporary European Cinema*, London: BFI/Hill, J. (1994) 'The Future of European Cinema: the economics and culture of pan-European strategies', in Hill et al, *Border Crossing: Film in Ireland, Britain and Europe*, Belfast: IIS/Queens University/BFI.

Scotland, for obvious reasons, has a somewhat schizophrenic relationship with Europe. As a 'Stateless Nation', to borrow David McCrone's terminology[4], welded to the rest of the United Kingdom by the 1707 Act of Union, Scotland is in turn part of the European Union and as such is eligible for EU schemes, including those in the Audio-Visual sector. But Scottish links with the continent have a long history and the rather fraught relationship between London and Brussels, fuelled by periodic xenophobic outbursts by Conservative M.P.'s, masks a specifically Scottish pro-European tradition. As historian Michael Lynch notes, the call by the Scottish National Party for an Independent Scotland within Europe in anticipation of the forging of an ever closer European Union in the 1990s, serves to re-establish one of the most important threads of continuity in Scottish history: 'Throughout the Middle Ages and beyond, Scottish soldiers, students, scholars and traders had tramped the roads of Europe and left their mark'[5].

This link between Scotland and Europe has left its imprint on Scottish film culture. We can identify a profound influence of certain trends in European art cinema in the work of Scottish film-makers of recent years including Bill Douglas, Bill Forsyth and Iain Sellar, and this identification with Europe will be discussed below.

Despite this special affinity, Scotland remains very much tied economically and politically to a Union dominated by England. However, in terms of the prevailing structures of audio-visual production, the UK is not so much characterised by an English hegemony as a Metropolitan one. The central institutions of the British film and television industries, like those of the British Government, are firmly located in London which is home to the handful of sources of production finance to which film-makers are forced to clamour — including Channel 4, British Screen, the BBC and the BFI Production Board. The major operating film studios and professional facilities, equipment hire, laboratories, editing suites, and dubbing studios are sited in and around the capital. The major independent producers, sales agents, distributors and industry bodies or groups are similarly based almost exclusively in and around Soho. Finally, the majority of acting and technical talent also resides within the fortress of the M25. This situation has generated a great deal of resentment north of the border, in that most Scots serious about pursuing a career in film are forced to emigrate to London.

In spite of the on-going structural weaknesses which characterise the British film industry as a whole, British film production has recently enjoyed what can only be described as a major boom. A total of 69 features were produced in Britain in 1993, a significant increase on the 47 in the previous year[6]. Moreover, this revival was sustained in 1994, with reports of the major studio complexes at Pinewood and Shepperton booked to capacity. This in turn has benefited Scottish film production with Scottish Screen Locations, an agency established in 1990 to promote Scotland as a location and production base for film-makers, reporting a staggering 14 features shot either wholly or partially in Scotland in 1994. This number includes four films registered as British, two television films, two North American productions, three British/North American co-productions, and three European films (two German and one Danish), and compares favourably

4. McCrone, D. (1992), *Understanding Scotland: The Sociology of a Stateless Nation*, London: Routledge.

5. Lynch, M. (1992), *Scotland: A New History*, London: Pimlico, pp. xx-xxi

6. Data from the *1995 BFI Handbook* (London: BFI, 1994), edited by Nick Thomas. The figure of 69 films is divided into 32 indigenous productions, 27 co-productions and 10 Hollywood-backed films made in Britain.

with previous years: seven productions for 1993, five for 1992 and four for 1991.

While this development is obviously crucial to the establishment of a film-making infrastructure in Scotland, it does not necessarily follow that an increase in the number of films being made implies a new vibrant indigenous Scottish cinema. For example, among the films assisted by Scottish Screen Locations from 1991-94 were the likes of *Diana: Her True Story*, and *Highlander III*, not to mention several foreign language productions. Over the last twenty five years Britain has been regularly used as a production base for American films such as the *Star Wars* and *Superman* trilogies and the first *Batman* film, directed by Tim Burton in 1989. Similarly, the current boom in studio production has been fuelled by the Hollywood majors, and if they decide that next year they would rather make films in German or Hungarian studios, then Britain will suffer accordingly.

But 1994 also provided some indication that Scottish film-making was, if not exactly thriving, at least showing some signs of life. The most exciting aspect of a rather dull Edinburgh Film Festival was the substantial number of Scottish works screened: a total of six new films, in addition to an unprecedented number of Scottish-funded short films. But what is more interesting, is the range of very different kinds of product that this selection of work embraces, which in turn raises important economic, aesthetic and cultural questions about what is actually meant by the term 'Scottish Film'.

The Edinburgh festival selection included three full length features: *Shallow Grave* (Richard Styles, 1987), a typical low budget (£1 million) British production, mainly funded by Channel 4, in partnership with the newly established Glasgow Film Fund; *Being Human* (Bill Forsyth, 1994), a $20 million US/UK co-production, backed by Warner Bros and written and directed by Bill Forsyth, still considered by many to be Scotland's premier film-maker; and *Ties*, a no-budget (i.e. self-financed) film, written, directed, and produced by newcomer Stephen Simpson. In addition to these, two television films were screened: *The Blue Boy*, directed by Paul Murton for BBC Scotland, and *Mairi Mhor*, a Gaelic language production written and produced by John McGrath, and directed by Mike Alexander, again for the BBC. Single dramas made for television regularly feature in selections of new British work at film festivals. This is partly a recognition that the old adage 'British cinema is alive and well and living on television' continues to have resonance, but occasionally TV films can be subsequently given a theatrical release on the basis of a strong showing at festivals. Among recent examples of this phenomenon are two films directed by Stephen Frears: *My Beautiful Laundrette* (Channel 4, 1985) and *The Snapper* (BBC, 1993). The sixth Scottish film shown at Edinburgh was *Brotherly Love*, a 50 minute graduation film by Angus Reid, a student at the Scottish Film School, and eight shorts were also programmed, three of which were funded by the ongoing BBC Scotland/Scottish Film Production Fund scheme 'Tartan Shorts'.

Significantly, all but three of these films were, arguably, made primarily for the small screen, while at least one of the three 'cinema' films, *Shallow Grave*, owes its existence to television finance. therefore, the impossibility of discussing questions of the production, distribution, and exhibition of contemporary Scottish film without acknowledging the central role of television in this process becomes clear. If we can argue that since the advent of Channel 4, British cinema has been effectively underwritten by television, then this is even more apparent with regard to such a peripheral entity as Scottish film. Television finance has also become extremely important in the wider European context. As John Hill has pointed out, 54% of European films produced in 1993 were backed to some extent by television (Hill, 1994).

Scotland was undoubtedly a beneficiary of the new broadcasting environment heralded by Channel 4. As John Caughie has shown, the transformation of Scottish film and television production which occurred during the 1980s was almost entirely due to Channel Four's commissioning policies. He describes 'the Channel Four effect' in the following way: 'At the most obvious level it has created the conditions for an expanding independent production sector. This in turn has created not only more, but more diverse films and programmes and representations. Perhaps even more importantly for the development of a film culture, it has allowed the work of the independent sector, and of a whole range of cinematic forms and national cinemas, to be seen. In the national peripheries, in Scotland and its peripheries, it is now possible to see work that ten years ago would not have been seen outside London, the major cities, or the occasional festival'[7]

Caughie also points out that in considering the emergence of this vibrant culture, one cannot afford to be too precious about cinema — either as an institution or as a means of exhibition. Television has not only been the major thrust behind the creation of a greater diversity of representation in Britain in the 1980s (benefiting not only Scottish, Welsh, Irish, Afro-Caribbean and Asian cultural interests), but it has also created audiences for these new works, new voices, new representations. In cultural terms, this has enabled the diversity and hybridity which marks contemporary British society to be reflected and nurtured. Moreover, a typical 'Film on Four' will be seen by far more people during a single screening on television than it will on a domestic cinema release.

Prior to 1982, independent Scottish film-makers existed on a diet of small scale commissions from television and the Government sponsored Films of Scotland. While one or two individuals such as Bill Forsyth and Charlie Gormley harboured ambitions to make features, the opportunities were few and far between, until the arrival of Channel Four[8].

This important television role has been augmented in Scotland by the BBC and Scottish Television. The BBC drama department in Glasgow has established a reputation as a producer of quality single dramas and series by acclaimed Scottish writers such as Peter Macdougall (*Just a Boy's Game, Down Where the Buffalo Go, Down Among the Big Boys*) and John Byrne (*Tutti Frutti, Your Cheatin' Heart*). STV, on the other hand, has been responsible for *Taggart*, the most popular networked Scottish drama series of recent years. However, the company has also invested in a range of Scottish feature films, including *Gregory's Girl* (1980) and *Comfort and Joy* (1994), both written and directed by Bill Forsyth; *A Sense of Freedom* (John Mackenzie, 1981), *Ill Fares the Land* (Bill Bryden, 1983), and *The Big Man*

7. Caughie, J. (1990), 'Representing Scotland: New Questions for Scottish Cinema', in Eddie Dick (ed.), From *Limelight to Satellite: A Scottish Film Book*, London: BFI/SFC.

8. Among the Scottish films subsequently backed by the Channel are *Scotch Myths* (Murray Grigor, 1982), *Hero* (Barney Platts Mills, 1982) — the Gaelic language feature film, *Another Time Another Place* (Michael Radford, 1983), *Living Apart Together* (Charlie Gormley, 1983), *Every Picture Tells a Story* (James Scott, 1984), *Heavenly Pursuits* (Charlie Gormley, 1986), *Blood Red Roses* (John McGrath, 1986), *Silent Scream* (David Hayman, 1989), *Venus Peter* (Iain Sellar, 1989), *Play Me Something* (Timothy Neat, 1989), *Prague* (Iain Sellar, 1992) and *Blue Black Permanent* (Margaret Tait, 1992).

(David Leland, 1990). But the BBC will also occasionally fund a film which, Channel Four style, will be given an opportunity to find an audience in the cinema before being broadcast. An example of such a project is *Easterhouse*, to be directed in 1995 by Gillies MacKinnon. While single dramas produced by BBC Scotland have to be approved by the London based commissioning editors responsible for the prime drama slots in the BBC's schedule, the Corporation is now moving towards a more devolved process of commissioning which, in theory, should lead to greater autonomy for Scottish drama projects.

Although the input of television companies such as Channel Four and the BBC is be vital to the survival of film-making in Scotland, recent years have seen the emergence of new sources of, primarily public, finance. In December 1989, the Secretary of State announced the creation of a Gaelic-language Broadcasting Fund. The fund, set at £9.5 million a year, is administered by Comataidh Telebhisein Gaidhlig (Gaelic Television Committee), based in Stornoway on the Isle of Lewis, under the direction of John Angus Mackay, and the first programmes funded by the CTG were broadcast in 1993. The fund's remit covered various genres of programme, from light entertainment, news broadcasts, religious and children's programmes, to documentary, but it has also made a contribution to Scottish drama.

While the CTG's flagship drama is the strictly small screen serial *Machair*, popularly described as the first gaelic soap, which is broadcast by STV at peak time, the CTG has also contributed to a handful of single drama projects including the short film *Sealladh* (The Vision, 1993) directed by Douglas Mackinnon; the feature *As An Eilan* (From the Island) (Mike Alexander, 1993) and the 60 minute TV film *Mairi Mhor* (1994). By virtue of being shot in the Gaelic language, these films engage unambiguously with the history and culture of the Scots Gaels.

The existence of the fund raises some interesting questions. While it has prompted a revival of interest in the Gaelic language, and a reduction in hostility towards Gaelic programming by anglophone Scots, it is also the case that many non-Gaelic speaking Glasgow based producers have since rushed to learn the language in order to offer programme proposals to the CTG[9]. So here we have an example of a cultural revival driven largely by an economic imperative, which further complicates questions of identity and authenticity in the field of audio-visual culture.

Moving beyond the television sector, the one body which is directly committed to nurturing film-making in Scotland is the Scottish Film Production Fund. The SFPF was set up in 1982 by the Scottish Film Council and the Scottish Arts Council with a brief to take a leading role in building an indigenous Scottish film industry[10]. Since its inception, the fund has grown substantially from an initial budget of just £80,000 to £340,000 by 1993/94, provided through subventions from the Scottish Office Education Department, Channel Four, and BBC Scotland[11]. This enabled the SFPF to provide more than £280,000, in support mainly for feature film development — 17 projects are listed in the Fund's 1993/94 annual report, in production funding for short films, with some additional grants for post production and industry related events. As the fund grew,

9. Petrie, D. (1995), 'The Scottish Audience' in Petrie and Willis (eds.), *Television and the Household*, London: BFI.

10. Lockerbie, I. (1990), 'Pictures in a Small Country: The Scottish Film Production Fund' in Eddie Dick (ed.) *From Limelight to Satellite: A Scottish Film Book*, London, BFI/SFC.

11. Information from *The Scottish Film Production Fund: Annual Report and Financial Statements, 1993/94.*. These debates have both been generated by the writing of Colin McArthur. See for example 'In Praise of a Poor Cinema', *Sight and Sound*, August 1993, and 'Low Budget Cinema Column', in *Scottish Film*, Issue 9, Third Quarter, 1994.

so did the necessity for proper full time administration, and this resulted in the appointment of a full time director in 1989.

In the twelve years of its existence, the SFPF has contributed to over 70 Scottish film projects including features, documentaries, animation, and shorts. During the 1980s, due mainly to limited resources, the fund tended to concentrate on documentaries, supporting works by Rosie Gibson, Brian Crumlish, Dianne Tammes and Paul Murton among others. However, as the fund has grown, so has its ability to contribute to feature films, and this trend is likely to continue[12].

Since 1993, the SFPF has also administered the Glasgow Film Fund, increasing by £150,000 a year the amount of money available for Scottish film-making. The first award made by the fund was to the feature *Shallow Grave*, directed by Danny Boyle and shot primarily in a custom built warehouse set in Glasgow. The film was a great success at the 1994 Cannes Film Festival, and was subsequently sold to several major territories. This makes it likely that the Glasgow Film Fund will recoup its investment, significantly increasing the size of the fund for future years.

In addition to features, the SFPF has expanded its involvement in short films, which traditionally have received little assistance[13] although, during the 1990s, this area of production has also been addressed largely through the successful 'Tartan Shorts' scheme. In 1993 the first three films to be produced under this initiative, co-funded by BBC Scotland, and guaranteed a television 'window', were premiered at the Edinburgh International Film Festival. One of these, *Franz Kafka's It's a Wonderful Life* (Peter Capaldi), subsequently won a BAFTA award for best short. The second three films produced in 1994 have consolidated this strong start, and the scheme is assured for at least the next three years. Current budgetary levels for the 'Tartan Shorts' stands at around £40,000 per film.

The SFPF has also contributed to the production and/or post production of a range of other short projects, in partnership with other funding bodies such as the BFI Production Board and even the Scottish Film Council. Indeed, the SFC currently supports a substantial number of first time film-makers through its 'First Reels' scheme, although the awards provided are tiny. The fund does help to nurture new talent, occasionally producing some noteworthy achievements. Atmospherically photographed in stark monochrome tones, Peter Mullan's *Close*, for example, is a shocking tale of urban paranoia and violence, which at times evokes Roman Polanski's 1960s classic *Repulsion*.

Arguably, short films are now the real bedrock of contemporary Scottish film-making despite being chronically under-valued as an aesthetic form in their own right, and generally regarded by film-makers, critics, and audiences alike as essentially apprentice works, leading to the 90 minute feature. Yet no-one would argue in the same way that the short story or the prose poem has somehow less integrity than the novel. The constraints attached to short film-making are of a different order from features: shorts are necessarily more impressionistic, with little room for character development, and often requiring some kind of 'punch-line' for narrative resolution. Yet they can be highly poetic and direct, condensing ideas, and encouraging brevity and economy. In Scotland, they are also distinguished by the fact that that they are fully fundable from indigenous sources. Given

12. Among those assisted over the years are *Living Apart Together* (Charlie Gormley, 1982), *Every Picture Tells a Story* (James Scott, 1984), *Play Me Something* (Timothy Neat, 1989), *Venus Peter* (Iain Sellar, 1989), *Silent Scream* (David Hayman, 1990), *Prague* (Iain Sellar, 1992), *Blue Black Permanent* (Margaret Tait, 1993) and *As An Eilean* (Mike Alexander, 1993).

13. op.cit., Lockerbie, I. 1990

the importance, both economic and cultural, of nurturing some kind of on-going film-making practice in Scotland, Scottish shorts deserve appropriate levels of critical engagement and support[14].

While the structures necessary to build and sustain film-making in Scotland do exist, films are still far from abundant, and consequently debate still rages around questions such as 'if Scotland had a cinema what should it look like?'. A great deal of writing about Scottish film tends to be prescriptive, first rejecting certain cultural representations[15], and then exploring what might replace them[16]. An attempt to identify suitable forms of representation was central to an event at the Glasgow film theatre, entitled 'Desperately Seeking Cinema: What Kind of Scottish Film-Making do we want?', and comprising a seminar, an informative dossier, and a series of films. However, rather than presenting examples which Scottish film might emulate, the event instead appeared to be a programme of the selectors' favourite films.

Despite the expansion in Scottish production since the 1980s the terrain is still being contested, as recent debates in publications such as *Sight and Sound* and *Scottish Film* testify. The most vociferous critic of current film-making in Scotland is Colin McArthur whose arguments for the necessity of a 'Poor Scottish cinema' are at odds with what he regards as the inappropriate commitment of the SFPF (and by extension the SFC), to narrative-based storytelling derived from Hollywood film practice, coupled with an emphasis on market-driven production strategies which not only drives up costs but also fails to address the more pressing cultural and social questions to which an indigenous Scottish cinema ought to be committed.

McArthur addresses much of his argument to the relationship between funding practices and aesthetic forms, and proscribes the notion of low budget, and indigenously-oriented films. While I do not share his views on the inappropriateness of current production strategies, the fact remains that when resources are limited, certain strategic priorities must be established. However, the thrust of the recent funding initiatives has arguably addressed the necessity of finding an audience, increasing the possibility of expanding resources. The lesson of *Shallow Grave* (1987) is a salutary one in this respect — a tightly plotted thriller, it is precisely the kind of well-made low budget film which stands a good chance of making a reasonable return on its £1 million budget, given its critical reception at the Cannes, Edinburgh, Dinard, and London film festivals. Yet the decision of the Glasgow Film Fund to invest its entire first year's budget in a single production is heavily criticised by McArthur as an inappropriate use of limited funds.

Perhaps the most controversial funding decision made by the SFPF was their substantial contribution to Iain Sellar's *Prague* — almost £140,000 invested over two years. The film, set in the Czech capital and largely backed by French money, was a commercial failure, and had difficulty securing a British distributor. While the propriety of investing such a large proportion of the fund in single production is certainly questionable, the decision was also criticised in that the film had only the slenderest connection with Scotland; apart from writer/director Sellar, and producer

14. McArthur, C. (1994), 'The Cultural Necessity of a Poor Celtic Cinema', in Hill et al (eds.), *Border Crossing: Film in Ireland, Britain and Europe*, Belfast: IIS/Queens University/ BFI.

15. McArthur, C. (ed.) (1982), *Scotch Reels: Scotland in Cinema and Television*, London: BFI.

16. op.cit., Caughie, J., 1990

Chris Young, only one member of the cast, Alan Cumming, is a Scot, and the bulk of the £2 million budget came from France.

Prague is of course an easy target for criticism, given that the other leading characters are played by Bruno Ganz (German) and Sandrine Bonnaire (French), making it something of a 'Euro-pudding', nevertheless, it does attempt to tell a genuinely European story. Cumming plays a young Scot who travels to Prague in the hope of finding a fragment of film which shows his grandparents attempting to escape from the Nazis, while being rounded up for transportation to the gas chambers. In his own quiet and tangential way, Sellar uses the quest to implicate Scotland in European history, and this, in turn, raises important questions about the nature of contemporary European identity. Sellar's slightly detached, impressionistic style reflects the European art cinema tradition, rather than the more popular dynamic narrative-based Hollywood approach.

Similar comments could well be made about Bill Forsyth's *Being Human*, an episodic tale of a man's struggle to be reunited with his family. This film too is widely regarded as a failure, in that it was unable to recoup the $20 million invested by Warner Bros. The narrative covers five different historical periods, each featuring a character called Hector, played by Robin Williams. But Forsyth's rather downbeat handling of the text was at odds with that of Warner who expected another *Local Hero*. The already considerable tensions intensified during the editing stage when the studio reduced Forsyth's initial cut from 2hrs 40mins to 85 minutes. Neither version proved popular in previews, so Forsyth produced a third, adding a voice-over to help bind the sections together. This final version, lasting just over 2 hours, was released in America in May 1994, where it made little impact.

Again, part of the problem is that Forsyth, like Sellar, has made a film in the European art cinema tradition, and by any standards a $20 million art movie is an anachronism. It is certainly not what a commercial Hollywood studio such as Warners bargained for, and the resulting tensions are visible in the film's structure. The decision to choose an American (Teresa Russell) to provide the voice-over, for example, sits uncomfortably with such a quintessentially European subject, for *Being Human*, like *Prague*, shows an attempt to situate Scotland firmly within European history, and although the final segment is located in contemporary New York/New Jersey, within the logic of the narrative this setting is merely the culmination of centuries of European wandering or searching.

It is tempting to suggest that *Being Human* might have been a much better film had it been made on a low budget. The most powerful moments centre around relationships, which do not require major resources, and the film might have stood a greater chance of finding a modest audience appropriate to a low budget venture.

Steve McIntyre has argued convincingly for the viability of such a low budget Scottish cinema, while avoiding the ideological posturing of Colin McArthur. He writes: 'It is important to note that low-budget film-making is not just a financial but also an aesthetic imperative: films like *Swoon* (1991), *Poison* (1990), *Slacker* (1991), *Edward II* (1991), *Man Bites Dog* (1992) work well not despite their budget but precisely because they are produced cheaply. If there is one defining characteristic of low-budget film-making it is that it dissolves the distinction between commercial film-making and "cultural film-making"; it is a meeting ground'[17].

Of course, the US examples cited are not 'Hollywood' productions, but independent films, made outside the dominant structures of the American industry, and as such owe more to the traditions of European art cinema than to the commercial and aesthetic practices of Hollywood. Moreover, if one takes seriously Colin MacCabe's assertion that Channel Four's contribution to British cinema amounts to a subsidy — 'a parafiscal levy on British television revenues'[18] — then Scottish cinema begins to take on very much the character of non-commercial European art cinema, supported primarily by a combination of Channel 4 and public funding via the SFPF and the BFI.

Moreover, while current Scottish films may embrace a diversity of subject matter, both historical and contemporary, inward and outward looking, attempts to articulate the 'Europeanness' of the Scots identifies a tendency which suggests a viable avenue for further exploration, and which brings us back to the beginning of this essay. Re-exploring Scotland's relationship with Europe, both past and present, allows a space for the articulation of an identity, itself necessarily hybrid, diverse, and outward looking — eschewing equally the regressive and parochial tropes of popular representation, and the essentialist embattled posture associated with British Europhobia.

17. McIntyre, S. (1994), 'Vanishing Point: Feature Film Production in a Small Country', in Hill et al (eds.), p.106
18. MacCabe, C. (1992), 'Subsidies, Audiences, Producers' in Duncan Petrie (ed.), *New Questions of British Cinema*, London: BFI.

Timetravel and European film
Wendy Everett

European film is fascinated by time, and shaped by a desire to return to the past, by an almost obsessive need to explore and interrogate memory and the process of remembering, apparently convinced that therein may be found the key to present identity. Of course, given Europe's overwhelming preoccupation with the past, its tendency to evaluate the present from a historical perspective or, as Baudrillard puts it, to '...operate in the uncanny realm of the *déjà vu* and the glaucous transcendence of history'[1], it is hardly surprising that its cinema should reflect this concern. Moreover, at a time when films are being used in the search for identity by individual nations fearing both a European takeover and increased American hegemony, cinema itself is also under threat, so that a search for its own filmic identity, and an evaluation of its cinematic heritage must be recognised as part of this wider exploration of history. European cinema has become increasingly self-conscious, engaged in endless retrospective and introspective examination. Again, the concerns of European nations and films coincide.

Given the fundamental European belief that we are our past, or that 'time is a condition for the existence of our "I"'[2], then memory, the thread which links us to our past, is ultimately what gives us coherence and identity:

> Our memory is our coherence, our reason for feeling, even our action. Without it, we are nothing[3].

Indeed, as earlier essays in this book have shown, concern with memory, history and identity emerges as one of the specificities or defining characteristics of European cinema. Memory and identity are seen as inseparable, and this essay will investigate their centrality in contemporary European cinema, and will suggest ways in which film itself may be seen to constitute a privileged medium for their expression, focusing in particular on the most personal of all representations of history: autobiographical film. Finally, it will examine the role cinema plays not merely in recalling, but in actually structuring our images of the past, possibly influencing the very process of remembering.

From the earliest days of cinema, film-makers were concerned with portraying the past, whether through literary adaptations, or through recreations of historical events. The vivid immediacy of the filmic image, which was later combined with memory trigger devices such as real news footage, authentic radio broadcasts, popular songs and music from the period being recalled, revealed film's unique ability to transport the spectator effortlessly through time and space. Cinema, it was clear, was the ideal time machine.

As we have seen, cinema's preoccupation with time and memory remains. However, Sorlin suggests certain significant changes in the way it presents the past, distinguishing between films made in the first half of the century, whose representations of history were essentially static, and later ones, where the past is understood as ongoing process or enquiry[4].

1. Baudrillard, J. (1988), *America*, London: Verso, p.84.
2. Tarkovsky, A. (1989), *Sculpting in Time: Reflections on the Cinema*, translated by Kitty Hunter-Blair, London: Faber and Faber, p.57.
3. Buñuel, L. (1982), *My Last Breath*, translated by Alfred A. Knopf, London: Fontana, pp.4-5
4. Sorlin, P. (1991), *European Cinemas, European Societies, 1939-1990*, London: Routledge, p.175.

The alternative discourse of the second approach, marked by its personal and critical tone, characterises, he suggests, 'historical' films of the 1970s and 1980s, such as *Stavisky* (Resnais, 1974), Hitler, *Ein Film aus Deutschland* (Hitler a Film from Germany, Syberberg, 1977), and *Rosa Luxemburg* (Von Trotta, 1987); films which affirm that all history is subjective, a matter of individual viewpoint, and which present remembering as an open-ended and continually changing process of reassessment. This treatment may be recognised as central to Kluge's *Die Patriotin* (The Patriot, 1979) in which a young history teacher struggles to unearth the fragmented and conflicting moments of Germany's past, so that it can re-member its identity (literally, for the film opens with the voice of a solitary knee journeying through the spatial and temporal construct of Germany), and thus be healed. And this notion of remembering as a process which allows understanding, development and a positive move forwards, is also fundamental to the autobiographical films at which we shall be looking.

For Sorlin, the move from objective to subjective representation of history in film reflects the influence of the more intimate language of television[5], and his thesis is attractive. However, there are equally — or even more — compelling arguments to support the notion that such treatment of the past is a function of cinematic discourse; the result of film's increasing awareness of its own structual affinity with time.

After all; film itself is fashioned from time; a quality recognised by Tarkovsky in *Sculpting in Time*, whose title refers both to the centrality of time and memory in the creation of identity, and to the fabric of film itself. Indeed, because so many filmic effects rely on the rhythmic variations of editing and camera movement, many contemporary directors, including Bergman, Straub, Duras, Delvaux and Robbe-Grillet, have asserted that film relates more closely to music than to any other art form. Tarkovsky, in fact, takes this argument a stage further:

> If one compares cinema with such time-based arts as, say, ballet or music, cinema stands out as giving time visible, real form[6].

In other words, the organisation of time is basic to any film, providing both its compositional dynamic and its narrative expression.

Tarkovsky's identification of cinema's unique ability to give time a *visible* and *real* form is significant because, despite the evident importance of the musical analogy, feature films generally present a narrative. They therefore involve the creation of complex temporal relationships between story (*histoire*) and discourse (*récit*), and discourse and narrator: the time of the telling and the time of the events being described: the creation of one time in another time[7]. Narrative discourse subverts the chronological sequence of story, involving temporal distortions which are expressed in film by such devices as flashback and flashforward, and various forms of linking, embedding, or alternation[8].

Temporal shifts are entirely normal in literature and, given Tarkovsky's comments about the director's task being to sculpt in time (p. 63), one would expect them to be at least as normal in film. However, here we touch upon a fascinating feature of film, which has traditionally been presented as a weakness: its lack of tense system. In other words, there is nothing inherent in cinematic images to indicate whether they are past,

5. Ibid., pp.173-187
6. op.cit.,Tarkovsky,A.,1989, p.118.
7. Metz, C. (1968), *Essais sur la signification du cinéma, tome 1*, Paris: Klincksieck, p.27.
8. Genette, G. (1980), *Narrative Discourse: An Essay in Method*, translated by Jane E. Lewis, Oxford: Blackwell, pp. 29-32

present or future[9]. Unlike the verb, which immediately situates us on a temporal axis, the filmic image has only one tense: 'Everything is always in the present in the cinema'[10]. It is in the nature of the filmic image to be perceived by the spectator as actually taking place, as occurring in the continuous present[11].

This highlights an interesting paradox: if cinema has no tense system[12], and if what we see on screen is automatically read as occurring in the present[13], how is it possible for filmic discourse to create the endlessly shifting tenses and viewpoints which are essential to narrative, and to modernist, self-conscious narrative in particular? How, in other words, can film be thought to constitute an ideal medium for the expression of time and memory?

Doubts about the ability of film to treat subjective reality and express personal viewpoint, have traditionally been used to justify the theory that autobiography, the most personal of all forms of discourse — informed, as it is, by the director's 'I', as well as his/her eye, and characterised by its endlessly shifting viewpoint and entirely subjective vision — could never become a genre suited to the cinema. And yet, as we have seen, European film is increasingly concerned with the exploration of personal vision, and with a quest for self-knowledge. Within the self-conscious and intimate portrayal of history as process and change acknowledged by Sorlin, autobiographical, and semi-autobiographical films have flourished dramatically. Some indication of the importance of this new filmic genre is provided by the following (selective) list of recent examples. These are given chronologically to support the idea that autobiographical film is actually gaining in popularity: *El Espiritu de la Colmene* (*Spirit of the Beehive*, Victor Erice, Spain, 1973); *Amarcord* (Federico Fellini, Italy, 1974); *Zerkalo* (*Mirror*, Andrey Tarkovsky, USSR, 1974); *Diabolo Menthe* (*Peppermint Soda*, Diane Kurys, France, 1975); *La Notte di San Lorenzo* (*Night of the Shooting Stars*, Paolo & Vittorio Taviani, Italy, 1981); *Fanny och Alexander* (*Fanny and Alexander*, Ingmar Bergman, Sweden, 1982); *Mit Liv Som Hund* (*My Life as a Dog*, Lasse Hallströn, Sweden, 1985); *Hope and Glory* (John Boorman, England, 1987); *Au revoir les enfants* (Louis Malle, France, 1987); *Chocolat* (Claire Denis, France, 1988); *Cinema Paradiso* (Giuseppe Tornatore, Italy, 1988); *Distant Voices, Still Lives* (Terence Davies, England, 1988); *Toto le héros* (*Toto the Hero*, Jaco van Dormael, Belgium, 1991); *Jacquot de Nantes* (Agnès Varda, France, 1991); *Un Nos Ola Leuad* (*One Full Moon*, Endaf Emlyn, Wales, 1991); *The Long Day Closes* (Terence Davies, England, 1992); *Biódagar* (*Movie Days*, Fridrik Fridriksson, Iceland, 1994); *Caro Diario* (*Dear Diary*, Nanni Moretti, Italy, 1994); *Hin helgu vé* (*The Sacred Mound*, Hrafn Gunnlaugusson, Iceland, 1994); *Portrait d'une jeune fille de la fin des années 60, à Bruxelles* (Chantal Akerman, 1994); *JLG/JLG* (Godard, France, 1994).

Different as these films may be, what they share is the desire of each director to explore very personal memories, not as part of a pleasant and reassuring nostalgia trip, but in order to understand some central, often repressed, and frequently painful, memory. They share not only the conviction that film provides a privileged medium for the exploration and interrogation of past identity, through its 'capacity for penetrating beyond the veils drawn by time'[14]; but also, that film can actually bring

9. Gaudréault, A. & F. Jost (1990), *Le Récit cinématographique*, Paris: Editions Nathan, p.101
10. Laffay, A. (1964), *Logique du cinéma*, Paris: Masson, p.16.
11. op.cit., Metz, C., 1968, p.18
12. Henderson, B. (1983), 'Tense, Mood and Voice in Film', in *Film Quarterly* (Fall), Berkeley, p.6
13. op.cit., Metz, C., 1968, p.18
14. op.cit., Tarkovsky, A., 1989, p.133

about the process of remembering, with the corollary of understanding and healing which alone permits personal change and development. Such a widely held conviction brings us back to the question of how film achieves this, particularly given its lack of tense and its problems in expressing subjective states of mind.

At its simplest level, lack of filmic tense can of course be overcome by the inclusion of certain codes or devices which film has developed to indicate temporal shifts: visual codes such as dissolves or fades, are used in conjunction with linguistic pointers such as voice-over or intertitles, to signal the slightest deviation from chronology. Nowhere is this more clearly illustrated than in the classical handling of flashback, cinema's own way of portraying remembered events. The flashback inserts an element from the narrative past into the narrative present, thus juxtaposing different moments of cinematic reference. To avoid ambiguity and possible confusion, in classical narrative the temporal status, and the start and finish of the flashback, must be clearly signalled. By way of example, let us consider Marcel Carné's *Le Jour se lève* (Daybreak, 1939); a film of great temporal complexity, whose essentially circular structure is composed of a series of flashbacks which occur between the moment when the hero (Jean Gabin) commits a murder, and his own suicide the following dawn. Through the flashbacks, we come to understand his reasons, and are forced to completely revise our initial reading of the incident. The starting point for each of the flashback sequences is a different object, which acts as a memory trigger for the hero but whose narrative and symbolic significance we, the spectators, will only gradually come to understand. In order to ensure that the spectators could cope with such complexity, the start and end of each flashback is extensively signalled: dissolve, music, voice-over (for instance, 'It seems only yesterday...') as well as contrasting lighting and costume, simultaneously warn of the change of tense.

If, however, the coding frame is removed, it becomes clear that what the flashback really portrays is the conjunction of entirely disparate filmic segments, each of which appears to depict actually occurring events, in the present tense. Changing tense in film is not a matter of movement from one discrete temporal category to another, but of the creation of a process or continuum, in which spatial and temporal transition are inseparable. For example, in *Hiroshima mon amour* (1959), Alain Resnais revolutionised the concept of flashback, by removing all temporal indicators. Cutting directly from present to past without warning, refusing to allow even the sound track to support time shifts, Resnais moves from a linguistic notion of time to one which is entirely cinematic. In so doing, he creates a film which functions as memory itself, since the painful process of recalling suppressed memories is always unpredictable, fragmentary, and partial. Unlike the memories which form *Le Jour se lève*, these are without logical pattern or structure. Resnais's concern is with the process of remembering and the way that past and present are not discrete, but continually impinge, one upon the other.

Modernist cinema recognises that far from being a clumsy way of handling temporal shifts, a poor imitation of its linguistic equivalent, flashback is a profoundly sophisticated recreation of the process of remembering; the 'tasting of the madeleine'. We do not remember in the

past tense, but in a flash of past as present; temporal categories are not discrete, our memories are part of the way we see and experience the present. We move constantly back and forth through time, and our viewpoint is constantly shifting.

Thus, the nature of filmic discourse equips it to deal with current notions of memory as process, and — essentially — as change. Moreover, this very mobility, itself the specificity of the filmic image, suggests a further way in which film is able to deal with memory. Our comparison this time is not between film and language, but film and photograph. Examining Bazin's claim that the photograph achieves an ontological status through its ability to imprint a mimetic image of perceived reality, Barthes maintains that photographs provide evidence that what we see once existed; the that-has-been, or the having-been-there of the object depicted endows the photograph with an assumed past tense[15]. Film, on the other hand, presents images which are in constant flux, each in turn effacing and interrogating the previous one. Thus, the photographic referent of film constantly shifts, and its images, perpetually drawn towards different views, do not provide proof of past existence. The tense of film is thus perceived as present, as actually happening, by virtue of the constant flow of images[16].

The distinction is important, for since the photograph freezes time, Barthes suggests, it blocks memory and cannot therefore bring about understanding, an essential component of remembering[17]. The essential mobility of film, on the other hand, allows it to function as memory. This theory is clearly demonstrated in *Paris, Texas* (Wenders, 1984).

Paris, Texas, like *Hiroshima mon amour*, is a film about identity and the process of remembering. Its hero, Travis, has suppressed the memory of certain traumatic events which caused him to abandon his young son, Hunter, and to embark on a solitary journey through the desert, in search of his lost identity. When Travis is found by his brother, his only possession is a photograph of a plot of land he has bought in Paris, Texas, in the belief that this is where he was conceived. The photograph represents his existence and his identity, and constitutes both the objective and the starting point of his journey. However, the photograph is static, it can neither restore memory[18], nor transfer grief into mourning, its active equivalent[19]. The photograph is isolated from the present by its tense.

The central point of the film, the moment at which Travis does begin the slow and painful process of remembering, and of discovering his identity, is a sequence in his brother's house when a home movie is being projected. In other words, Wenders presents us with a flashback which is itself a film screened within the diegesis, and is therefore able to achieve a sense of anteriority without assuming narrative omniscience. It is through this screening that Travis and Hunter rediscover their father/son relationship, as they gradually recall and acknowledge their shared past: (static) grief becomes (active) mourning.

But what Wenders is doing here is even more complex, for the film/flashback provides an examination of the nature of film language and tense: functioning as present within present, filmic memory parallels the process of remembering; it becomes part of that process, unlike Travis's photograph, locked forever in its past. Memory is movement; it is flux.

That Wenders intends this sequence to function as a comment on the

15. Barthes, R. (1984), *Camera Lucida: Reflections on Photography*, translated by Richard Howard, London: Fontana, p.91.

16. Ibid., p.89

17. Sontag, S. (1979), *On Photography*, London: Penguin Books, p.23

18. op.cit., Barthes, R., 1984, p.91.

19. op.cit., Sontag, S. 1979, p.73

nature of filmic language is underlined by the essential self-consciousness of the film-in-a-film device, and the way the home movie repeatedly draws our attention to the camera. Moreover, just as Travis and Hunter are spectators of their memory process, so too we, as spectators of *Paris, Texas*, are directly involved in this process of remembering, since Wenders refuses to provide discrete boundaries between the two films; music from the one being used as accompaniment to the other, and so on. There is no attempt to enclose the home movie in the past (as in classical treatment of flashback); instead, Wenders both makes use of, and draws our attention to, the way it functions as continuous process.

The essentially dynamic nature of filmic time, endlessly explored in self-conscious modernist films, accounts for their frequent representation of memory and the search for identity as journeys: the moving camera both reflects and constructs narrative impetus, and comments on and explores temporal mobility. In *Paris, Texas*, Travis's initial journey, in search of what he believed to be the source of his identity, his past, represented by the photograph, proves futile because it is a past which is isolated from his present. However, the home movie sequence, by forcing him to recognise memory as part of his present identity, enables him to set out on another journey, this time a fruitful one, to find his wife. Once this has been achieved, and mother and son have been reunited, the essential remembering and healing processes are complete, and he is free to resume his journey. As he drives away from us, although we do not know where or why he is going, we know that he is making a positive move towards the future.

The self-conscious recognition of the process of memory reflected in the linking of memory and journey is widespread in contemporary European films. In Agnès Varda's *Sans toit ni loi* (Vagabond, 1985), for example, following Mona's journey through an icy winter landscape, the camera constantly pans from right to left, a visual indication of the unseen narrator's attempts to retrace and to understand the period and events leading to Mona's death (with which the film opens). The device is particularly common in autobiographical films, where the formal filmic structures are exposed through the narrative linking of memory and journey. In Claire Denis's *Chocolat* (1988), for example, the recollection of France's childhood, which constitutes the main part of the narrative, is set within the frame of a brief car journey, whose direction across the screen is from left to right. When a series of words and actions, occurring between the driver of the car and his young son, act as memory triggers, and the physical journey to the past becomes a mental one, the camera changes position, and the car appears to move from right to left, as it is itself transported into the memory sequence. For the spectator as well as the protagonist the narrative past of flashback is then perceived as narrative present, until a sound jolts us back from remembered time, and there is a corresponding switch of camera direction. At this stage, France has re-experienced the painful and confusing events of her childhood, but this time, with the dual vision and understanding of the adult gaze; her anticipated physical journey is no longer necessary, and like Travis in *Paris, Texas*, she moves on, out of the frame and away from us, towards her future. Several of the other autobiographical films listed above also use a journey structure both as illustration of the memory process (linked through spatial and temporal movement) and as a contextualisation of cinematic language. *Cinema Paradiso*, for instance, involves frequent switching from adult to child or adolescent narrator (all three being represented within the diegesis), and these temporal shifts function within a partial frame of a return journey to Sicily, which both echoes and finally permits a reconciliation of the time shifts. Again, the final reconciliation of present and past, is set in motion by a film; this time, a compilation which Alfredo (the projectionist) had made for Toto, using all the clips which the priest had judged unsuitable for public consumption. This 'film' adds a further self-conscious comment, in that the censored clips it contains reflect the memories which Toto had censored, whose recollection is essential if he is to move forward. It is possible that recalling such suppressed memories is a central aspect of autobiography.

Au revoir les enfants opens with a train journey which appears to represent simply the child's return to school, but whose cold blue/grey colours, and repeated images of the child imprisoned within tightly framed shots, isolated and impotent, also constitute Malle's painful return to his past. This reading is supported by Malle's admission that he had originally intended to include a voice-over to explain that the film was biographical, but that he found that the opening sequence made any such intervention unnecessary[20]. On the other hand, Malle's voice at the end of the film, acknowledging his childhood guilt and its constant presence in his adult life, provides a return to the present; a new present, since it now includes the past.

Since autobiographies are structured by memory, narrative coherence is not a major concern. It is an interesting comment on the general misunderstanding of the genre that critical writings about such films often condemn their 'shapelessness'. One such example is to be found in the comment by Icelandic film critic Gisli Einarsson that the structure of *Movie Days* 'does not allow for much drama, and there is no storyline to speak of'[21]. There is, of course, something almost random about the process of remembering, in that any sound or smell may suddenly transport the adult back to childhood, and the very mobility of filmic images can capture this quality. In *The Long Day Closes*, for example, Davies's camera slips through time, seeming to chance upon a patch of light on a snow-covered window ledge, or on a patterned carpet, and then simply remaining there; slowly remembering and giving the spectator time to remember similar moments; requiring of the spectator a creative response, a complicity.

Since autobiographical time is subjective, chronology is relatively unimportant. External time may intrude, via radio broadcasts or newsreels, but it functions only to provide a context, and it too is liable to be distorted by memory, existing only on those occasions when it has a direct relevance to the child. Equally, the events themselves must be recognised as part truth, part fiction, for that is the nature of memory.

20. Malle, 1993, pp.181–182.
21. Einarsson, G. (1995), in Cowie, P. (ed.) (1995), *Variety International Film Guide 1995*, London: Hamlyn.
22. op.cit., Buñuel, L., 1982, p.5.

Our imagination, and our dreams, are forever invading our memories: and since we are all apt to believe in the reality of our fantasies, we end up transfering our lies into truths. Of course, fantasy and reality are equally personal, and equally felt, so their confusion is a matter of only relative importance[22].

Imagination, dreams, and fantasy constitute a child's reality, likewise film whose images, no matter how strange, will be perceived as both real and present, has the unique ability to capture this quality. Examples of this include the sailing ship in Bud's daydream, whose spray actually drenches him, in *The Long Day Closes*, and the moving statues and anchor being dragged across the carpet in front of Alexander, in *Fanny and Alexander*.

Therefore, despite their apparent mimetic precision, what these films depict is still a personal vision; their 'realism' exists not to underwrite historical authenticity, but to recreate a lost world. As Tarkovsky acknowledges, film is a privileged medium because it can portray the world exactly as it is remembered, without recourse to the elusive ambiguity of words[23]. Therefore, far from being ill-equipped to explore the subjective landscape of history, film has a unique ability to do so, hence its centrality in the current European quest for memory and identity.

But what of the changing viewpoints which characterise autobiography: the slippage between adult and child's vision; the coincidence of personal involvement and ironic distance? What we are talking about here is the subverting of perspective, which Lejeune sees as essential to autobiography, since the adult's voice must intervene from time to time to ensure that the child's viewpoint requires a dual reading. In other words, the meaning(s) lie within the oscillating and uncertain relationship between the two voices[24]. This is another area which has generally been presented as impossible to portray on film, largely because of the technical problems in producing a narrative which is purely subjective[25], or the belief that film automatically portrays an objective viewing, 'the world seen without a self'[26]. That film can show personal vision, we have now established. If we consider the constantly shifting viewpoint, and the simultaneous involvement and detachment which feature in all of the films listed earlier, we discover that, once again, the endless mobility of the camera, and the apparent realism of the images, are well able to express such complexities. Terence Davies, for instance, in *The Long Day Closes*, allows his camera to take quite literally an ironic overview of the tightly knit universe of his childhood. He does this in a sequence where the camera looks vertically down at the child, and then executes a single continuous tracking shot from right to left, encompassing child, cinema, church, and school, before returning (impossibly) to its starting point. Spatial logic is destroyed, child and adult worlds exist simultaneously, and the director also comments, through the impossibility of the shot, on the ultimate impenetrability of childhood.

In conclusion, European films have become increasingly self-referential, using filmic structures to draw attention to the means whereby their fiction is created; to make the spectator aware of the process of filmic narrative. Part of this is a recognition and an exploration of the specificities of the medium, not least its ability to deal with time. Thus, as we have seen, the process of remembering is often set within a journey structure in which temporal and spatial elements are expressed as movement, in order to reveal and interrogate the process of remembering; and if, as I have intimated, the process of time travel is part of cinema's natural construct, then we may expect to find film itself as the defining myth at the end of such journeys. Film provides not only the starting point and the vehicle

23. op.cit., Tarkovsky, A., 1989, p.4

24. Lejeune, P. (1980), *Je est un autre*, Paris: Editions du Seuil, p.30.

25. Orr, J. (1993), *Cinema and Modernity*, Cambridge: Polity Press, p.10

26. McConnell, p.113?

in this European time travel phenomenon, but also the final destination. In Alain Robbe-Grillet's ludic film-puzzle, *Trans-Europ-Express* (1966), the journey continues endlessly, in both directions. Moreover, it is a journey in which the spectator is actively implicated, by virtue both of the open-ended nature of the experience (for if memory is process there can be no conclusion); and because the narrative is fragmentary, containing silences and blanks which the spectators must fill in, not on the basis of what is shown, but by searching within their memories and themselves filling in the blanks. The importance of autobiographical explorations of personal memory in contemporary Europe therefore lies in the direct involvement they require of each spectator, who must also remember and reassess. Autobiographical films have an endless capacity for irony and reflection; they constitute a self-conscious quest on the part of both director and spectator and, within the wide references they draw on, cinema itself occupies a central position. Writing about the Douglas autobiographical trilogy, and *Distant Voices, Still Lives*, Orr comments upon this aspect:

> ...as autobiographical memory films reconstructing the past, they draw on the heritage of the British documentary, the highly charged poetic power of John Grierson and Humphrey Jennings. But they do so because they are part of the wider age of modern European cinema. It seems impossible to conceive of Douglas's work without the prior example of Bresson (...). The delicate interwoven memories in Davies's picture of working class Liverpool after the war, his bittersweet family chronicle, seem impossible to imagine without the emotional intensity of Bergman or the complex memory narratives of Resnais and Fellini. The work of both directors builds on the modern cinema as such[27].

Shared experiences therefore shape the identities which autobiographical films interrogate, as they shape the response and reading of the spectator, and account for the sense of recognition which greeted these films, right across Europe.

Essentially, then, the films acknowledge European memory and myth, while also showing the centrality of film itself within this myth. European film and European identity are inextricably linked; both are part of the same journey through time.

27. op.cit., Orr, J., 1993, p.47

Bibliography

Anderson, B. (1991), *Imagined Communities*, London: Verso.

Auty, M. & N. Roddick (1985), *British Cinema Now*, London: BFI.

Berry, D. (1994), *Wales & Cinema: The First Hundred Years*, Cardiff: University of Wales Press.

Buss, R. (1989), *Italian Films*, London: B. T. Batsford Ltd.

Curran, J. and V. Porter (1983), *British Cinema History*, London: Weidenfield & Nicolson.

Drummond, P., R. Paterson & J. Willis (eds.) (1993), *National Identity and European Cinema*, London: BFI.

Eddie, D. (ed.), *From Limelight to Satellite: A Scottish Film Book*, London: BFI/SFI.

Edwards, J. (ed.) (1985), *Language, Society and Identity*, Oxford: Blackwell.

Elsaesser, T. (1989), *New German Cinema: A History*. London: BFI.

Featherstone, M. (ed.) (1990), *Global Culture*, London: Sage.

Friedman, L. (ed.) (1993), *British Cinema and Thatcherism*, London: UCL Press.

Gelner, E. (1983), *Nations and Nationalism*, Oxford: Blackwell.

Hayward, S. (1993), *French National Cinema*, London and New York: Routledge.

Hill, J. et al (eds.), (1994), *Border Crossing: Film in Ireland*, Belfast: IIS/Queens University/BFI.

Hopewell, J. (1986), *Out of the Past: Spanish Cinema after Franco*, London: BFI.

Horton, A. & M. Brashinsky (1992), *The Zero Hour: Glasnost and Soviet Cinema in Transition*, Princeton, New Jersey: Princeton University Press.

Lawton, A. (1992), *Kinoglast: Soviet Cinema in Our Time*, Cambridge: Cambridge University Press.

McArthur, C. (ed.) (1982), *Scotch Reels: Scotland in Cinema and Television*, London: BFI.

Miller, D. (1994), *Don't mention the War: Northern Ireland, Propaganda and the Media*, London: Pluto Press.

Petrie, D. (ed.) (1992), *New Questions of British Cinema*, London: BFI.

Petrie, D. (ed.), (1992), *Screening Europe: Image and Identity in Contemporary European Cinema*, London: BFI.

Orr, J. (1993), *Cinema and Modernity*, Cambridge: Polity Press.

Rockett, K., L. Gibbons & J. Hill (1988), *Cinema and Ireland*, London: Routledge.

Sorlin, P. (1991), *European Cinemas, European Societies, 1939-1990*, London: Routledge.

Taylor, R. & D. Spring (eds.), *Stalinism and Soviet Cinema*, London and New York: Routledge.

Turim, M. (1989), *Flashbacks in Film: Memory and History*, New York and London: Routledge.

Whyte, J. (1991), *Interpreting Northern Ireland*, Oxford: Clarendon Press.